The Secret Teachings of Warren Buffett

Capiace Wilson

Published by Financierpro Publishing, 2023.

THE SECRET TEACHINGS OF WARREN BUFFETT

First edition. March 16, 2023.

Copyright © 2023 Capiace Wilson.

ISBN: 979-8215405260

Written by Capiace Wilson.

Table of Contents

Preface

Warren Edward Buffett, commonly known as Warren Buffett, is an American business magnate, investor, and philanthropist. He was born on August 30, 1930, in Omaha, Nebraska, and is currently the Chairman and CEO of Berkshire Hathaway, a multinational conglomerate holding company. He is widely regarded as one of the most successful investors in history, and his net worth is estimated at over $100 billion. Early Life and Education - Warren Buffett was born to Leila and Howard Buffett. His father was a stockbroker and ran a small investment partnership. Buffett developed an interest in business and investing at a young age and began investing in stocks at the age of 11. He would often spend hours at his father's office, studying financial reports and reading financial newspapers. Buffett attended the University of Nebraska, where he studied business and economics. After graduating, he went on to study at the Columbia Business School, where he learned under the legendary investor Benjamin Graham. Graham's investment philosophy of value investing, which involves buying stocks that are undervalued and holding them for the long term, had a profound impact on Buffett's investment philosophy. In 1956, Buffett formed his first investment partnership, Buffett Associates, Ltd. The partnership was based on the principles of value investing and focused on buying stocks that were undervalued. Over time, the partnership's success attracted more investors, and by 1962, it had grown to $7.2 million in assets under management. In 1965, Buffett acquired a textile manufacturing company called Berkshire Hathaway. Initially, he had planned to use the company as a vehicle for investment, but he soon realized that the company's textile business was in decline. He then began to acquire other companies under the Berkshire Hathaway umbrella, using the profits from these companies to invest in other businesses. Over the years, Buffett has made many successful investments, including in companies such as Coca-Cola, American Express, and Gillette. He is known for his long-term investment strategy, which involves buying stocks and holding them for years or even decades. He has also been known to invest in undervalued companies and companies with strong competitive advantages. Buffett's investment success has earned him the nickname "The Oracle of Omaha." He has consistently been ranked among the wealthiest people in the world, and his net worth has grown significantly over the years. In addition to his successful career in business and investing, Buffett is also known for his philanthropic efforts. In 2010, he and Bill and Melinda Gates launched The Giving Pledge, an initiative that encourages billionaires to pledge to donate at least half of their wealth to charitable causes. Buffett has also pledged to donate most of his wealth to philanthropic causes. In 2020, he donated $2.9 billion to various charities, bringing his total charitable giving to over $37 billion. Buffett has also been involved in various philanthropic initiatives, including the Buffett Foundation, which focuses on education, healthcare, and poverty alleviation. He has also donated billions of dollars to the Bill and Melinda Gates Foundation, which works to improve global health and reduce poverty. Despite his enormous wealth and success, Buffett has maintained a relatively low profile throughout his life. He still lives in the same house in Omaha that he bought in 1958 for $31,500, and he has been married to his second wife, Astrid Menks, since 2006. Buffett is also known for his frugal lifestyle. Despite being one of the wealthiest people in the world, he famously drives a modest car and eats at fast-food restaurants. He has also said that he plans to give away most of his wealth and leave very little to his heirs. In terms of his personal beliefs, Buffett has been a vocal advocate for progressive taxation and has been critical of the growing wealth inequality in the United States. He has also been a supporter of the Democratic Party and has donated to various Democratic candidates over the years. Legacy and Influence - Warren Buffett's investment success and philanthropic efforts have made him a highly influential figure in the business world. Many investors and entrepreneurs look to him as a role model and try to emulate his investment strategies. Buffett's investment philosophy of value investing has also had a significant impact on the investment world. Many investors have adopted his approach of buying undervalued stocks and holding them for the long term. He has also emphasized the importance of investing in companies with strong competitive advantages and has warned against investing in companies with high levels of debt. In addition to his investment philosophy, Buffett's philanthropic efforts have also had a significant impact. His commitment to giving away most of his wealth has inspired other billionaires to do the same, and The Giving Pledge has become a powerful force for philanthropy. In summary, Warren Buffett is one of the most successful investors in history and has had a significant impact on the business world. His investment philosophy of value investing and his long-term approach to investing have inspired many investors and entrepreneurs. His philanthropic efforts have also had a significant impact, and he has become a leading voice for philanthropy and charitable giving. Despite his enormous wealth and success, Buffett has maintained a modest and frugal lifestyle and has remained committed to giving away most of his wealth to charitable causes. Berkshire Hathaway is a multinational conglomerate holding company that is involved in a wide range of businesses and industries. The company's portfolio of subsidiaries includes companies in sectors such as insurance, retail, energy, manufacturing, and more. Here are some examples of Berkshire Hathaway's businesses: Insurance: Berkshire Hathaway is primarily known for its insurance subsidiaries, including GEICO, Berkshire Hathaway Reinsurance Group, and Berkshire Hathaway Primary Group. These subsidiaries offer a range of insurance products, including auto insurance, property insurance, and more.

Manufacturing: Berkshire Hathaway owns several manufacturing companies, including Precision Castparts Corp, which produces metal components for aircraft engines and other industrial applications. Other manufacturing subsidiaries include Forest River, a maker of recreational vehicles, and Clayton Homes, a manufacturer of mobile homes. Retail: Berkshire Hathaway owns several retail companies, including Nebraska Furniture Mart, a large home furnishings store, and Borsheims, a jewelry retailer. The company also owns Dairy Queen, a chain of fast-food restaurants, and See's Candies, a chocolate and candy retailer. Energy: Berkshire Hathaway owns several energy companies, including Berkshire Hathaway Energy, which operates a portfolio of energy companies, including utilities and renewable energy companies. The company also owns a stake in Canadian oil and gas company Suncor Energy. Financial Services: Berkshire Hathaway owns several financial services companies, including Berkshire Hathaway HomeServices, a real estate brokerage, and Berkshire Hathaway Specialty Insurance, which offers specialized insurance products. In addition to these businesses, Berkshire Hathaway also holds significant investments in a variety of publicly traded companies, including Apple, Coca-Cola, and American Express. In summary, Berkshire Hathaway is a diversified holding company with a wide range of subsidiaries and investments across various industries. The company's businesses range from insurance and manufacturing to retail and energy, and it is well-known for its long-term investment approach and its chairman, Warren Buffett.

"If you don't find a way to make money while you sleep, you will work until you die." Warren Buffett

Introduction

Warren Buffett's investment strategies were influenced by several people, but the most significant was his mentor, Benjamin Graham. Graham was an economist, investor, and professor at Columbia Business School, where Buffett studied. Graham is widely regarded as the father of value investing, a philosophy that seeks to buy stocks at a discount to their intrinsic value. Buffett learned the principles of value investing from Graham and went on to apply them throughout his career. In this chapter, we will explore the life and work of Benjamin Graham and how his teachings influenced Warren Buffett's investment strategies. Benjamin Graham was born in London in 1894 and moved to New York City with his family when he was one year old. He attended Columbia University and graduated with a degree in economics in 1914. After graduation, he worked for several Wall Street firms, including Newburger, Henderson & Loeb and the Northern Pipeline Company. In 1928, Graham began teaching at Columbia Business School, where he taught courses on security analysis and investing. His teaching focused on the principles of value investing, which he developed in his book, "Security Analysis," co-authored with David Dodd in 1934. Graham's investment philosophy was based on the idea that the market is not always efficient and that stocks can be mispriced, presenting opportunities for investors to buy them at a discount to their intrinsic value. He believed that a stock's intrinsic value was based on its earnings power and that investors could determine a stock's intrinsic value by analyzing its financial statements. Graham's approach to investing involved identifying companies with strong fundamentals, such as a low price-to-earnings ratio, a high dividend yield, and a low debt-to-equity ratio. He believed that investors should focus on the long-term prospects of a company rather than its short-term fluctuations in stock price. Buffett was first introduced to Graham's investment philosophy when he read "The Intelligent Investor," one of Graham's most famous books. The book emphasized the importance of value investing and provided a framework for analyzing stocks.

Buffett was immediately drawn to Graham's approach and began applying his principles to his own investment strategies. Buffett went on to study under Graham at Columbia Business School, where he learned the ins and outs of value investing. He later described Graham as his mentor and credited him with teaching him everything he knew about investing. Buffett applied Graham's principles to his investment partnership, Buffett Associates, Ltd., which he formed in 1956. The partnership focused on buying undervalued stocks and holding them for the long term. Buffett's investment philosophy was based on the idea that a stock's value was based on its intrinsic value, and that investors could make money by buying stocks at a discount to their intrinsic value. Buffett's investment strategies proved to be highly successful, and he quickly became one of the most successful investors in history. He is known for his long-term approach to investing and his ability to identify undervalued companies with strong fundamentals. Some of Buffett's most successful investments include Coca-Cola, American Express, and Gillette. He is also known for his investments in financial institutions, including Goldman Sachs and Bank of America. Buffett's investment strategies have had a significant impact on the investment world, and many investors have tried to emulate his approach to investing. His success as an investor has made him a highly influential figure in the business world, and he is widely regarded as one of the most successful investors of all time. Warren Buffett's investment strategies were heavily influenced by his mentor, Benjamin Graham. Graham's investment philosophy of value investing emphasized the importance of buying stocks at a discount to their intrinsic value and focusing on the long -term prospects of a company. Value investing has become a popular investment strategy among investors who want to follow in Buffett's footsteps and achieve long-term success. Value investing offers several advantages over other investment strategies. For one, it is a methodical approach to investing that is based on fundamental analysis rather than emotions or market trends. Value investors look for companies that are trading at a discount to their intrinsic value, which can provide a margin of safety against market volatility. Another advantage of value investing is that it tends to be less risky than other investment strategies. By focusing on companies with strong fundamentals, value investors are more likely to invest in companies that are financially stable and have a competitive advantage in their industry. This can help to mitigate the risks of investing in the stock market. However, there are also some disadvantages to value investing. One of the biggest drawbacks is that it can be difficult to find undervalued companies in today's market. With the rise of algorithmic trading and the increasing efficiency of the market, it can be challenging for investors to find companies that are truly undervalued. Another disadvantage of value investing is that it can require a lot of patience. Value investors typically hold onto their investments for the long term, which means that they may need to wait years before seeing a return on their investment. This can be difficult for investors who are looking for quick gains. Value investing is an investment strategy that emphasizes the importance of buying stocks at a discount to their intrinsic value. The principles of value investing were developed by Benjamin Graham, who was Warren Buffett's mentor. Buffett applied Graham's principles to his own investment strategies and achieved tremendous success as an investor. Value investing offers several advantages over other investment strategies, including a focus on fundamental analysis and the potential for less risk. However, there are also some disadvantages to value investing, including the difficulty of finding undervalued companies and the need for patience. Overall, value investing is a strategy that has stood the test of time and has been used successfully by many investors. While it may not be the right strategy for everyone, it can be a valuable tool for investors who are looking to achieve long-term success in the stock market. The Graham and Dodd approach is an investment philosophy that emphasizes the importance of fundamental analysis in evaluating potential investments. This approach was developed by Benjamin Graham and David Dodd, two professors at Columbia Business School, and is based on the principles outlined in their book "Security Analysis." The Graham and Dodd approach emphasizes the importance of analyzing a company's financial statements to determine its intrinsic value. This involves evaluating a company's assets, liabilities, earnings, and cash flow to determine its true worth. The approach also emphasizes the importance of a margin of safety, which is the difference between the intrinsic value of a company and its current market price. The key principles of the Graham and Dodd approach include - Margin of Safety: The margin of safety is the difference between the intrinsic value of a company and its current market price. This is a critical component of the Graham and Dodd approach, as it provides a buffer against unexpected events or market fluctuations.

Fundamental Analysis: The Graham and Dodd approach emphasizes the importance of fundamental analysis in evaluating potential investments. This involves analyzing a company's financial statements to determine its intrinsic value, as well as its competitive position, management team, and industry dynamics. Long-Term Horizon: The Graham and Dodd approach is focused on long-term investing and emphasizes the importance of patience and discipline in achieving investment success. Diversification: The Graham and Dodd approach also emphasizes the importance of diversification, as it can help to reduce risk and enhance returns over time. The Graham and Dodd approach has influenced many successful investors, including Warren Buffett, who has referred to Graham as his mentor and has credited the approach with his investment success. Buffett has adopted many of the key principles of the Graham and Dodd approach in his own investing, including the focus on intrinsic value and the margin of safety. One of the key tenets of the Graham and Dodd approach is the importance of intrinsic value. This is the true worth of a company, based on its underlying assets, earnings, and cash flow. The approach involves analyzing a company's financial statements to determine its intrinsic value, and then comparing this value to its current market price. The approach also emphasizes the importance of a margin of safety, which is the difference between the intrinsic value of a company and its current market price. This provides a buffer against unexpected events or market fluctuations, and helps to ensure that investors are buying stocks at a discount to their true worth. The Graham and Dodd approach is also focused on long-term investing and emphasizes the importance of patience and discipline in achieving investment success. The approach encourages investors to take a long-term view and to avoid making impulsive decisions based on short-term market fluctuations. Finally, the Graham and Dodd approach emphasizes the importance of diversification in building a successful investment portfolio. This involves spreading investments across a range of asset classes, industries, and geographies to reduce risk and enhance returns over time. Overall, the Graham and Dodd approach is a fundamental analysis-based investment philosophy that emphasizes the importance of intrinsic value, a margin of safety, a long-term horizon, and diversification. By adopting these principles, investors can build a successful investment portfolio that is focused on long-term growth and profitability. The Graham and Dodd model is a valuation method that is used to estimate the intrinsic value of a stock. This model was developed by Benjamin Graham and David Dodd, who are the fathers of value investing. The formula for the Graham and Dodd model is as follows: Intrinsic Value = EPS x (8.5 + 2g) x (4.4 / Y) Where: EPS = Earnings Per Share

g = Expected Growth Rate of Earnings

Y = Current Yield on AAA Corporate Bonds

The formula calculates the intrinsic value of a stock based on its earnings per share (EPS), the expected growth rate of earnings (g), and the current yield on AAA corporate bonds (Y). The EPS is the company's net income divided by the number of outstanding shares. This is an important factor in the model, as it reflects the profitability of the company. The expected growth rate of earnings (g) is an estimate of the rate at which the company's earnings will grow in the future. This is a key factor in the model, as it reflects the potential for future profitability and growth. The current yield on AAA corporate bonds (Y) is used as a benchmark for the risk-free rate of return. This is important in the model, as it reflects the opportunity cost of investing in the stock market versus investing in risk-free assets. The formula also includes a multiplier of 8.5 + 2g, which reflects the relationship between the price-to-earnings (P/E) ratio and the expected growth rate of earnings. The multiplier is based on the assumption that a stock's P/E ratio should be equal to its growth rate plus a constant factor of 8.5. Finally, the formula includes a second multiplier of 4.4 / Y, which reflects the relationship between the yield on AAA corporate bonds and the risk premium for investing in the stock market. The multiplier assumes that the expected return on stocks should be higher than the yield on risk-free assets, to compensate investors for the additional risk. By plugging in the relevant variables, investors can use the Graham and Dodd model to estimate the intrinsic value of a stock. If the intrinsic value is higher than the current market price, the stock may be considered undervalued and a good investment opportunity. It's important to note that the Graham and Dodd model is just one valuation method and should not be used in isolation. Investors should also consider other factors, such as the company's competitive position, management team, and industry dynamics, when evaluating potential investments. Overall, the Graham and Dodd model provides a framework for investors to estimate the intrinsic value of a stock based on its earnings, growth rate, and risk profile. By using this model, investors can identify undervalued stocks that have the potential for long-term growth and profitability. Graham's first rule of investing is to always seek a margin of safety. In other words, investors should always aim to purchase stocks at a discount to their intrinsic value to minimize their risk of loss. This margin of safety provides a buffer against unexpected events or market fluctuations and helps to ensure that investors are buying stocks at a discount to their true worth. The margin of safety is calculated as the difference between the intrinsic value of a security and its market price. By determining a security's intrinsic value, investors can estimate the price they should be willing to pay for it. This can be done using various valuation methods, such as the Graham and Dodd model, which takes into account the company's earnings per share (EPS), the expected growth rate of earnings (g), and the current yield on AAA corporate bonds (Y). Once the intrinsic value has been determined, investors should aim to purchase the security at a price that provides a margin of safety. This means that the market price should be lower than the intrinsic value, by a sufficient amount to provide a buffer against unexpected events or market fluctuations. Graham's second rule of investing is to always be patient and disciplined. This means that investors should avoid making impulsive decisions based on short-term market fluctuations or emotional reactions to news events. Instead, investors should take a long-term view and focus on the underlying fundamentals of the companies in which they invest. This involves conducting thorough research and analysis to identify companies with strong competitive positions, solid management teams, and long-term growth potential. Once these companies have been identified, investors should hold onto their investments for the long term, even in the face of short-term market fluctuations. By adhering to these two rules, Graham believed that investors could minimize their risk of loss and achieve long-term investment success. These principles are still widely used today and are considered essential for any investor looking to build a successful investment portfolio. In addition to his two rules of investing, Graham also developed several other important principles for successful investing, such as the importance of diversification, the need for a disciplined approach to investing, and the value of a contrarian perspective. These principles continue to influence investors today and are a testament to Graham's legacy as one of the most influential thinkers in the field of investment finance. Benjamin Graham, known as the "father of value investing," developed several key principles for successful investing throughout his career. These principles continue to influence investors today and are considered essential for anyone looking to build a successful investment portfolio. Here are 7 significant investment tips from Benjamin Graham: Invest with a margin of safety: Graham believed that the key to successful investing was to always seek a margin of safety. This means investing in securities that are trading below their intrinsic value, to minimize the risk of loss. Conduct thorough analysis: Graham believed in the importance of fundamental analysis in evaluating potential investments. This involves analyzing a company's financial statements, management team, competitive position, and industry dynamics to determine its true worth. Focus on the long-term: Graham believed that successful investing requires patience and discipline. Investors should take a long-term view and focus on the underlying fundamentals of the companies in which they invest, rather than reacting to short-term market fluctuations. Diversify your portfolio: Graham believed in the importance of diversification in building a successful investment portfolio. This means spreading investments across a range of asset classes, industries, and geographies to reduce risk and enhance returns over time. Don't follow the crowd: Graham believed that investors should avoid following the crowd and instead take a contrarian perspective. This means looking for opportunities in stocks that are undervalued or out of favor with the market. Embrace volatility: Graham believed that volatility was a natural part of investing and should be embraced, rather than feared. Investors should be prepared for market fluctuations and be willing to hold onto their investments through periods of volatility. Maintain discipline: Graham believed that successful investing requires a disciplined approach. Investors should have a clear investment strategy, stick to their principles, and avoid making impulsive decisions based on emotion or short-term market fluctuations. Overall, Graham's investment tips emphasize the importance of fundamental analysis, a long-term perspective, diversification, contrarian thinking, and discipline. By following these principles, investors can minimize their risk of loss and achieve long-term investment success.

Chapter 1
Value Investing

Value investing is an investment strategy that involves buying stocks that are undervalued by the market. The goal of value investing is to buy stocks that are trading below their intrinsic value, which is determined by analyzing the company's financial statements and other fundamental data. The idea behind value investing is that the market does not always accurately reflect the true value of a company, and that investors can profit by buying stocks when they are trading at a discount to their intrinsic value. The origins of value investing can be traced back to the work of Benjamin Graham and David Dodd, who wrote "Security Analysis," a seminal work on investment analysis, in 1934. Graham and Dodd believed that stocks could be analyzed like bonds, by calculating their intrinsic value based on the company's financial statements. Graham and Dodd's approach to value investing involved looking for companies that had strong fundamentals, such as a low price-to-earnings ratio, a high dividend yield, and a low debt-to-equity ratio. They believed that investors should focus on the long-term prospects of a company rather than its short-term fluctuations in stock price. The principles of value investing can be broken down into three main categories: financial analysis, business analysis, and market analysis. Financial analysis is the cornerstone of value investing. The goal of financial analysis is to determine the intrinsic value of a company by analyzing its financial statements. Financial analysis involves looking at a company's income statement, balance sheet, and cash flow statement to determine its financial health. The income statement provides information on a company's revenue and expenses and can be used to calculate its earnings per share. The balance sheet provides information on a company's assets, liabilities, and equity, and can be used to calculate its book value per share. The cash flow statement provides information on a company's cash inflows and outflows and can be used to calculate its free cash flow per share. Business analysis involves looking at a company's operations and industry to determine its long-term prospects. Business analysis involves looking at a company's products and services, its management team, its competitive position, and its industry trends A company's products and services should be in demand and have a competitive advantage over other companies in the industry. The management team should be experienced and have a track record of success. The company should have a strong competitive position in its industry, with barriers to entry that protect its market share. Finally, the industry should be growing and have favorable long-term prospects. Market analysis involves looking at the market's perception of a company's value. Market analysis involves looking at a company's price-to-earnings ratio, price-to-book ratio, and other metrics to determine whether the market is undervaluing or overvaluing the company. The price-to-earnings ratio is a measure of a company's stock price relative to its earnings. A low price-to-earnings ratio may indicate that the market is undervaluing the company, while a high price-to-earnings ratio may indicate that the market is overvaluing the company. The price-to-book ratio is a measure of a company's stock price relative to its book value. A low price-to-book ratio may indicate that the market is undervaluing the company, while a high price-to-book ratio may indicate that the market is overvaluing the company. One of the main advantages of value investing is that it is a long-term strategy that is based on the fundamentals of a company. Value investing is not focused on short-term fluctuations in stock price, but rather on the long-term prospects of a company. This means that value investors are more likely to hold onto their investments for a long period of time, which can help them avoid making impulsive decisions based on short-term market movements. By taking a long-term approach, value investors are able to ride out market volatility and focus on the underlying strengths of the companies they invest in. Another advantage of value investing is that it can be a more conservative approach to investing. By focusing on companies with strong fundamentals, value investors are less likely to invest in companies that are highly leveraged or that have volatile earnings. This can help to reduce the overall risk of their investment portfolio and potentially provide more consistent returns over time. Additionally, value investing can be a more affordable approach to investing. By focusing on undervalued companies, value investors may be able to find stocks that are trading at a discount to their intrinsic value. This means that they can potentially buy stocks at a lower price and capture greater returns when the market eventually recognizes the true value of the company. Despite its many advantages, there are also some potential drawbacks to value investing. One of the main challenges of value investing is finding undervalued companies in a market that is becoming increasingly efficient. As more investors adopt value investing strategies, it can become harder to find undervalued stocks that are not already priced correctly by the market. Another challenge of value investing is that it can require a lot of patience. Because value investors are focused on the long-term prospects of a company, they may need to hold onto their investments for many years before they see a return. This can be difficult for investors who are looking for more immediate returns on their investments. Value investing is a long-term investment strategy that emphasizes the importance of buying undervalued companies with strong fundamentals. While it can offer many advantages, such as a more conservative approach to investing and potentially greater affordability, it also comes with some challenges, such as the need for patience and the difficulty of finding undervalued companies in an efficient market. Overall, value investing can be a valuable approach to investing for investors who are willing to take a long-term view and focus on the underlying strengths of the companies they invest in.

Chapter 2
Long – Term Strategy

A long-term investment strategy is an investment approach that focuses on buying and holding investments for an extended period. The goal of a long-term investment strategy is to build wealth over time, with a focus on capital appreciation and income generation. Long-term investing is often contrasted with short-term investing, which focuses on buying and selling investments quickly to generate short-term profits. Long-term investors, on the other hand, are more interested in the long-term prospects of the investments they hold and are less concerned with short-term market fluctuations. One of the main benefits of a long-term investment strategy is that it allows investors to take advantage of the power of compounding. Compounding occurs when investment returns are reinvested back into the investment, allowing the investor to earn returns on both their initial investment and their investment returns. Over time, the power of compounding can lead to significant growth in an investment portfolio. Another benefit of a long-term investment strategy is that it can help investors avoid making impulsive decisions based on short-term market movements. By taking a long-term view, investors can focus on the underlying fundamentals of the investments they hold, rather than being swayed by short-term market fluctuations. In addition, a long-term investment strategy can help investors achieve their financial goals over time. By holding investments for the long term, investors can potentially generate more consistent returns, which can help them achieve their financial objectives, such as saving for retirement or building a college fund for their children. While a long-term investment strategy can offer many benefits, there are also some risks to consider. One of the main risks of a long-term investment strategy is that it requires patience and discipline. Investors who are focused on short-term gains may be tempted to sell their investments during periods of market volatility, which can lead to missed opportunities for long-term growth. Another risk of a long-term investment strategy is that it can be more difficult to adjust to changing market conditions. Investors who are committed to a long-term strategy may be less likely to make changes to their investment portfolio, even if market conditions suggest that a change is necessary. Finally, a long-term investment strategy may not be suitable for all investors. Depending on an individual's financial goals, risk tolerance, and investment time horizon, a short-term investment strategy or a combination of both short-term and long-term strategies may be more appropriate. If you are interested in implementing a long-term investment strategy, there are several steps you can take to get started. First, you will need to identify your investment goals and develop a plan for achieving them. This may involve setting specific financial targets, such as a retirement savings goal or a college fund target. Once you have identified your investment goals, you will need to develop a plan for achieving them. This may involve selecting investments that align with your investment goals and risk tolerance, and developing a long-term investment plan that includes regular contributions to your investment portfolio. In addition, you may want to consider working with a financial advisor who can help you develop a long-term investment plan that is tailored to your specific financial situation and goals. A financial advisor can also provide guidance and support as you navigate the ups and downs of the stock market and work towards achieving your long-term financial objectives. A long-term investment strategy is an investment approach that focuses on buying and holding investments for an extended period. By taking a long-term view, investors can potentially take advantage of the power of compounding and achieve more consistent returns over time. While there are risks associated with a long-term investment strategy, such as the need for patience and discipline, it can be a valuable approach to investing for investors who are willing to take a patient and disciplined approach to building their investment portfolio. When implementing a long-term investment strategy, it's important to consider factors such as your investment goals, risk tolerance, and investment time horizon. By developing a plan that aligns with your specific financial situation and goals, you can create a roadmap for achieving your long-term financial objectives. In addition to setting specific financial targets, a long-term investment strategy may involve selecting investments that are well-suited to your risk tolerance and long-term investment horizon. This may involve diversifying your investment portfolio across different asset classes, such as stocks, bonds, and real estate, to manage risk and potentially increase returns. Another key component of a long-term investment strategy is regular contributions to your investment portfolio. By contributing to your investment portfolio on a regular basis, you can potentially take advantage of dollar-cost averaging, which can help to reduce the impact of short-term market fluctuations on your investment returns. Ultimately, a long-term investment strategy can be a valuable approach to investing for investors who are willing to take a patient and disciplined approach to building their investment portfolio. While it may require some sacrifice and discipline in the short-term, a long-term investment strategy can help you achieve your financial goals and build lasting wealth over time.

Chapter 3
Timeless Wisdom

Benjamin Graham and David Dodd are two of the most influential figures in the history of finance and investing. Together, they wrote "Security Analysis" and "The Intelligent Investor," two of the most important books ever written on investing. Their timeless wisdom has helped generations of investors navigate the ups and downs of the stock market and build wealth over time. Graham and Dodd's investment philosophy was based on the principles of value investing. Value investing involves buying stocks that are undervalued by the market and holding onto them for the long term. The goal of value investing is to buy stocks that are trading below their intrinsic value, which is determined by analyzing the company's financial statements and other fundamental data. Graham and Dodd believed that investors should focus on the long-term prospects of a company rather than its short-term fluctuations in stock price. They believed that the market does not always accurately reflect the true value of a company, and that investors can profit by buying stocks when they are trading at a discount to their intrinsic value. One of the key tenets of value investing is the concept of a margin of safety. Graham and Dodd believed that investors should always seek to buy stocks that have a margin of safety, or a margin of error in their intrinsic value calculations. This can help to protect against losses if the market does not recognize the true value of the company. Graham and Dodd's approach to investment analysis involved looking for companies that had strong fundamentals, such as a low price-to-earnings ratio, a high dividend yield, and a low debt-to-equity ratio. They believed that investors should focus on the long-term prospects of a company rather than its short-term fluctuations in stock price. In "Security Analysis," Graham and Dodd outlined a detailed approach to investment analysis, including how to analyze a company's financial statements, how to value a company's stock, and how to construct a diversified investment portfolio. Their approach to investment analysis was based on the idea that investors should focus on the underlying fundamentals of a company, rather than trying to predict short-term market movements. By focusing on the long-term prospects of a company, investors can potentially take advantage of the power of compounding and achieve more consistent returns over time. Another key aspect of Graham and Dodd's investment philosophy was the importance of discipline and patience. They believed that investors should be disciplined in their investment approach and should only invest in companies that met their strict criteria for value. Graham and Dodd also emphasized the importance of patience when investing. They believed that investors should be willing to hold onto their investments for the long term, even if the market is volatile or if the company is experiencing short-term setbacks. Today, the principles of value investing, and Graham and Dodd's investment philosophy continue to be highly influential in the world of finance and investing. Many of the world's most successful investors, including Warren Buffett, have been influenced by Graham and Dodd's timeless wisdom and investment philosophy. In a world that is becoming increasingly focused on short-term gains and market speculation, Graham and Dodd's approach to investing offers a valuable counterbalance. By focusing on the long-term prospects of a company, and by having the discipline and patience to hold onto investments for the long term, investors can potentially achieve more consistent returns over time and build lasting wealth. Benjamin Graham and David Dodd were two of the most influential figures in the history of finance and investing. Their investment philosophy, based on the principles of value investing and long-term thinking, has helped generations of investors navigate the ups and downs of the stock market and build lasting wealth. Today, the wisdom of Graham and Dodd continues to be highly relevant, as investors continue to seek out a disciplined and patient approach to investing that is focused on the long-term prospects of a company. Their principles of value investing, which involve buying stocks at a discount to their intrinsic value and holding onto them for the long term, can help investors build wealth over time while managing risk. By focusing on the underlying fundamentals of a company, rather than being swayed by short-term market fluctuations, investors can potentially achieve more consistent returns over time. In addition, Graham and Dodd's emphasis on discipline and patience can help investors avoid making impulsive decisions based on short-term market movements. By having a clear investment strategy and sticking to it, investors can potentially avoid costly mistakes and achieve their financial goals over time. Overall, the timeless wisdom of Benjamin Graham and David Dodd serves as a reminder that investing is a long-term game, and that the key to success lies in having a disciplined and patient approach that is focused on the long-term prospects of a company. While the world of finance and investing may be constantly evolving, the principles of value investing, and long-term thinking continue to be highly relevant for investors who are seeking to build lasting wealth over time.

Chapter 4
Financial Statements

Analyzing a company's financial statements is a critical step in the investment process. Financial statements provide investors with valuable information about a company's financial health, including its revenues, expenses, assets, liabilities, and cash flows. By analyzing a company's financial statements, investors can gain insights into the company's profitability, liquidity, and financial stability, which can help them make informed investment decisions. Here are the key steps to analyze a company's financial statements: Step 1: Gather Financial Statements - The first step in analyzing a company's financial statements is to gather the necessary financial documents. This typically includes the company's balance sheet, income statement, and cash flow statement. These financial statements are typically available on the company's website or through the Securities and Exchange Commission's (SEC) EDGAR database. Step 2: Review the Income Statement - The income statement, also known as the profit and loss statement, provides information about a company's revenues and expenses over a specific period. When analyzing the income statement, investors should look for trends in revenue growth and profitability, as well as any changes in expenses. Key metrics to consider when analyzing the income statement include revenue growth, gross profit margin, operating profit margin, and net income. Investors should also review the footnotes to the financial statements, which provide additional information about the company's accounting policies and any unusual items that may have affected the income statement. Step 3: Examine the Balance Sheet - The balance sheet provides information about a company's assets, liabilities, and equity as of a specific date. When analyzing the balance sheet, investors should look for trends in the company's liquidity, solvency, and financial flexibility. Key metrics to consider when analyzing the balance sheet include current ratio, debt-to-equity ratio, and return on equity. Investors should also review the footnotes to the financial statements, which provide additional information about the company's accounting policies and any unusual items that may have affected the balance sheet. Step 4: Review the Cash Flow Statement - The cash flow statement provides information about a company's cash inflows and outflows over a specific period. When analyzing the cash flow statement, investors should look for trends in the company's operating cash flow, investing cash flow, and financing cash flow. Key metrics to consider when analyzing the cash flow statement include free cash flow, cash flow from operations, and cash flow from financing activities. Investors should also review the footnotes to the financial statements, which provide additional information about the company's accounting policies and any unusual items that may have affected the cash flow statement. Step 5: Analyze Financial Ratios - Financial ratios are useful tools for analyzing a company's financial statements. Ratios can be used to compare a company's performance to industry benchmarks or to other companies in the same sector. Some of the key financial ratios to consider when analyzing a company's financial statements include - Price-to-Earnings Ratio (P/E Ratio): This ratio compares a company's current stock price to its earnings per share. A high P/E ratio may indicate that the market is expecting strong growth from the company, while a low P/E ratio may indicate that the market is expecting weaker growth. Debt-to-Equity Ratio: This ratio compares a company's total debt to its total equity. A high debt-to-equity ratio may indicate that the company is highly leveraged and may be at risk of default, while a low debt-to-equity ratio may indicate that the company is financially stable. Return on Equity (ROE): This ratio compares a company's net income to its shareholder equity. A high ROE may indicate that the company is generating strong returns for its shareholders, while a low ROE may indicate that the company is not using its equity efficiently. Step 6: Conduct Additional Analysis - In addition to the steps outlined above, investors may also want to conduct additional analysis when analyzing a company's financial statements. This may involve: Examining Management Commentary: Many companies include management commentary or analysis in their financial statements. This can provide additional insight into the company's performance, strategy, and outlook. Conducting Industry Analysis: Investors may want to examine the company's financial statements in the context of its industry. This can involve comparing the company's financial ratios to industry benchmarks or analyzing industry trends that may impact the company's performance. Analyzing Non-Financial Factors: While financial statements provide important information about a company's financial health, there are also non-financial factors that may impact the company's performance. This may include factors such as market trends, regulatory changes, and competitive landscape. Using Financial Modeling: Some investors may choose to use financial modeling to analyze a company's financial statements. Financial modeling involves using mathematical formulas to forecast a company's future performance based on historical data. Analyzing a company's financial statements is an important step in the investment process. By reviewing the income statement, balance sheet, and cash flow statement, as well as conducting financial ratio analysis, investors can gain valuable insights into a company's financial health. In addition, investors may want to conduct additional analysis, such as examining management commentary, conducting industry analysis, analyzing non-financial factors, or using financial modeling, to gain a more complete understanding of the company's performance and prospects. By taking a thorough and disciplined approach to analyzing a company's financial statements, investors can make informed investment decisions that are based on solid financial data.

Chapter 5
Stock Value

Valuing a company's stock is an essential part of the investment process. There are several methods that investors can use to value a company's stock, each of which has its own advantages and disadvantages. In this chapter, we will explore the most common methods for valuing a company's stock. The price-to-earnings (P/E) ratio is one of the most widely used methods for valuing a company's stock. This ratio compares a company's stock price to its earnings per share (EPS). To calculate the P/E ratio, divide the current stock price by the company's EPS for the most recent 12-month period. The P/E ratio is a useful tool for comparing the value of one company's stock to another company's stock in the same industry. However, it should be noted that the P/E ratio may not accurately reflect a company's true value, as it does not take into account factors such as growth prospects, debt levels, and cash flow. The price-to-book (P/B) ratio is another commonly used method for valuing a company's stock. This ratio compares a company's stock price to its book value per share. To calculate the P/B ratio, divide the current stock price by the company's book value per share. The P/B ratio is useful for comparing the value of one company's stock to another company's stock in the same industry. However, it should be noted that the P/B ratio may not accurately reflect a company's true value, as it does not consider factors such as growth prospects, debt levels, and cash flow. Discounted cash flow (DCF) analysis is a more complex method for valuing a company's stock. This method involves estimating a company's future cash flows and discounting them back to their present value. To conduct a DCF analysis, investors must make assumptions about a company's growth prospects, profitability, and cash flow. DCF analysis is a useful tool for valuing companies that have predictable cash flows and growth prospects. However, it can be difficult to estimate these factors with accuracy, and small changes in assumptions can have a significant impact on the final valuation. The dividend discount model (DDM) is another method for valuing a company's stock. This method involves estimating the future dividends that a company is expected to pay and discounting them back to their present value. To conduct a DDM analysis, investors must make assumptions about a company's dividend growth rate, payout ratio, and discount rate. The DDM is a useful tool for valuing companies that pay regular dividends and have a history of increasing their dividend payouts. However, it may not be applicable to companies that do not pay dividends or have an inconsistent dividend payout history. The price-to-sales (P/S) ratio is a method for valuing a company's stock that compares its stock price to its revenue per share. To calculate the P/S ratio, divide the current stock price by the company's revenue per share for the most recent 12-month period. The P/S ratio is useful for comparing the value of one company's stock to another company's stock in the same industry. However, it should be noted that the P/S ratio may not accurately reflect a company's true value, as it does not consider factors such as growth prospects, debt levels, and cash flow. Valuing a company's stock is an important step in the investment process. There are several methods that investors can use to value a company's stock, each of which has its own advantages and disadvantages. It's important for investors to carefully consider these methods and choose the one that is most appropriate for the company they are analyzing. In addition to the methods discussed above, there are a few other factors that investors should consider when valuing a company's stock: Investors should consider the industry and market trends that may impact a company's performance and prospects. For example, a company operating in a high-growth industry may be more attractive to investors than a company operating in a stagnant industry. The quality of a company's management team is an important factor to consider when valuing its stock. Investors should look for companies with strong and experienced management teams who have a proven track record of success. Investors should consider the competitive landscape in which a company operates. A company with a strong competitive advantage, such as a unique product or service, may be more attractive to investors than a company that faces stiff competition. Economic conditions can have a significant impact on a company's performance and prospects. Investors should consider factors such as interest rates, inflation, and consumer confidence when valuing a company's stock. Valuing a company's stock is a complex process that requires careful analysis of a wide range of factors. There are several methods that investors can use to value a company's stock, each of which has its own advantages and disadvantages. By carefully considering these factors and using the appropriate valuation method, investors can make informed investment decisions that are based on solid financial data.

Chapter 6
Diversified Investment Portfolio

Constructing a diversified investment portfolio is essential for investors who want to achieve their long-term financial goals while managing risk. A diversified portfolio can help investors reduce their exposure to market volatility and increase the likelihood of achieving consistent returns over time. In this chapter, we will explore the key steps to construct a diversified investment portfolio. The first step in constructing a diversified investment portfolio is to determine your investment goals and risk tolerance. Your investment goals may include factors such as your desired rate of return, time horizon, and liquidity needs. Your risk tolerance will depend on your personal financial situation, including your income, expenses, and other financial commitments. Once you have determined your investment goals and risk tolerance, the next step is to develop an investment strategy. This will involve selecting the types of assets that you want to include in your portfolio, such as stocks, bonds, real estate, or commodities. It's important to remember that different asset classes have different risk and return characteristics, so it's important to select a mix of assets that are appropriate for your investment goals and risk tolerance. Asset allocation is the process of dividing your investment portfolio among different asset classes. The goal of asset allocation is to reduce your exposure to market volatility while increasing the likelihood of achieving consistent returns over time. There are several methods for determining the appropriate asset allocation for your portfolio, including the age-based method, which suggests that investors should allocate a higher percentage of their portfolio to stocks when they are younger and shift to bonds as they get older. Another method is the risk-based method, which suggests that investors should allocate their portfolio based on their risk tolerance. This may involve allocating a higher percentage of their portfolio to stocks if they have a higher risk tolerance, and a higher percentage to bonds if they have a lower risk tolerance. Once you have determined the appropriate asset allocation for your portfolio, the next step is to select investments within each asset class. This may involve selecting individual stocks, bonds, mutual funds, or exchange-traded funds (ETFs). It's important to diversify within each asset class, as this can help reduce your exposure to company-specific risk. For example, if you are investing in stocks, you may want to select a mix of large-cap, mid-cap, and small-cap stocks, as well as stocks in different industries. Finally, it's important to monitor and rebalance your portfolio on a regular basis. This may involve reviewing your portfolio at least once a year to ensure that it continues to align with your investment goals and risk tolerance. If your portfolio has drifted significantly from your target asset allocation, you may need to rebalance by selling some investments and buying others to bring your portfolio back into balance. Constructing a diversified investment portfolio is essential for investors who want to achieve their long-term financial goals while managing risk. By determining your investment goals and risk tolerance, developing an investment strategy, considering asset allocation, selecting investments within each asset class, and monitoring and rebalancing your portfolio on a regular basis, you can build a portfolio that is appropriate for your needs and that can help you achieve your long-term financial goals.

Chapter 7
Mutual Funds

The origins of mutual funds can be traced back to the early 19th century, when a group of Dutch investors created a vehicle called a "communal fund" to pool their money and invest in a variety of stocks and bonds. However, it wasn't until the early 20th century that the modern mutual fund industry began to take shape. In 1924, the first modern mutual fund, known as the Massachusetts Investors Trust, was created by investment banker Edward C. Johnson II. The fund was designed to allow small investors to gain exposure to a diversified portfolio of stocks and bonds, which was previously only available to wealthy investors. The Massachusetts Investors Trust was modeled after the investment trusts that were popular in the United Kingdom at the time. Unlike investment trusts, which were closed-end funds that traded on stock exchanges and had a fixed number of shares, the Massachusetts Investors Trust was an open-end fund that issued and redeemed shares daily. The Massachusetts Investors Trust was a success, and other investment companies soon followed suit. By the 1950s, the mutual fund industry had grown significantly, with assets under management reaching $2.5 billion. The mutual fund industry continued to grow throughout the second half of the 20th century, as more and more investors began to recognize the benefits of pooled investing. Mutual funds provided investors with access to professional management, diversification, and liquidity, which were previously only available to institutional investors. Today, the mutual fund industry is a major component of the global financial system, with trillions of dollars in assets under management. Mutual funds are available in a variety of asset classes and investment strategies, and they continue to provide individual investors with a convenient and cost-effective way to invest in the financial markets. Mutual funds are a popular investment option for individuals who want to gain exposure to a variety of asset classes, such as stocks, bonds, and real estate, without having to purchase individual securities. Mutual funds are managed by professional fund managers who use the pooled funds of many investors to purchase securities on their behalf. In this chapter, we will explore the best strategies for investing in mutual funds. The first step in investing in mutual funds is to determine your investment goals and risk tolerance. This will help you determine the types of mutual funds that are appropriate for your investment needs. Your investment goals may include factors such as your desired rate of return, time horizon, and liquidity needs. Your risk tolerance will depend on your personal financial situation, including your income, expenses, and other financial commitments. Once you have determined your investment goals and risk tolerance, the next step is to choose the right type of mutual fund. There are several types of mutual funds, each of which has its own investment objective and risk profile. Equity Funds: These funds invest in stocks and are suitable for investors who are willing to take on a higher level of risk to achieve higher returns. Fixed Income Funds: These funds invest in bonds and are suitable for investors who are looking for a lower-risk investment option that provides a steady stream of income. Balanced Funds: These funds invest in a mix of stocks and bonds and are suitable for investors who are looking for a balanced approach to investing. Index Funds: These funds track a specific market index, such as the S&P 500, and are suitable for investors who want to achieve returns that closely match the performance of the index. Sector Funds: These funds invest in a specific sector of the economy, such as technology or healthcare, and are suitable for investors who want to gain exposure to a specific sector. The expense ratio is the cost of managing a mutual fund and is expressed as a percentage of the fund's assets. It's important to consider the expense ratio when investing in mutual funds, as high fees can eat into your returns over time. Generally, index funds and passively managed funds have lower expense ratios than actively managed funds. When selecting a mutual fund, it's important to compare the expense ratios of similar funds to ensure that you are getting good value for your investment. When investing in mutual funds, it's important to evaluate the fund's past performance to get an idea of how it has performed in different market conditions. However, past performance is not a guarantee of future results, and investors should consider other factors, such as the fund's investment strategy and risk profile, when evaluating a mutual fund. Dollar-cost averaging is a strategy for investing in mutual funds that involves investing a fixed amount of money on a regular basis, such as monthly or quarterly. This can help investors avoid market timing and reduce the impact of short-term market fluctuations on their returns. Dollar-cost averaging can be an effective strategy for long-term investors who are looking to build a diversified portfolio over time. When investing in mutual funds, it's important to consider the fund's tax efficiency. This involves looking at the fund's tax structure and considering factors such as the fund's turnover rate, capital gains distributions, and tax implications of dividends. Investors should consider investing in tax-efficient funds, such as index funds, to minimize the impact of taxes on their returns. Investing in mutual funds can be a great way to gain exposure to a variety of asset classes without having to purchase individual securities. By determining your investment goals and risk tolerance , choosing the right type of mutual fund, considering the fund's expense ratio, evaluating the fund's past performance, practicing dollar-cost averaging, and considering tax efficiency, investors can build a well-diversified mutual fund portfolio that is appropriate for their needs. It's important for investors to remember that mutual fund investing involves risk and that past performance is not a guarantee of future results. It's important to conduct thorough research and due diligence when selecting mutual funds and to consult with a financial advisor or professional if necessary. Overall, mutual funds can be an effective tool for achieving long-term investment goals and managing risk. By following these strategies and staying disciplined, investors can build a diversified mutual fund portfolio that is tailored to their investment needs and risk tolerance. There are several ways to make money with mutual funds, including: Capital appreciation: One way to make money with mutual funds is through capital appreciation. When the value of the underlying securities in the mutual fund increases, the net asset value (NAV) of the mutual fund also increases. If an investor sells their shares in the mutual fund when the NAV is higher than when they purchased it, they will realize a capital gain. Dividend income: Many mutual funds pay regular dividends or distributions to their investors. These dividends can be reinvested back into the mutual fund, potentially increasing the investor's holdings over time. Interest income: Fixed income mutual funds invest in bonds or other fixed income securities, which generate interest income for the fund. This interest income is typically passed on to investors in the form of regular distributions. Professional management: Mutual funds are managed by professional portfolio managers who make investment decisions on behalf of the fund's investors. These managers use their expertise and market knowledge to select securities that they believe will generate the best returns for the fund's investors. Diversification: Because mutual funds invest in a variety of different securities, investors can achieve diversification within a single investment. This can help to reduce the overall risk of the portfolio and potentially increase returns over time. It's important to note that mutual funds also come with some risks, such as market risk and management risk. It's important for investors to carefully evaluate mutual funds and consider factors such as the fund's investment objective, fees and expenses, performance history, and risk profile before making an investment. A financial advisor or professional can help guide investors through the process of selecting mutual funds that are right for their investment goals and risk tolerance. Mutual funds are a popular investment option for beginners because they offer instant diversification and professional management. However, with so many mutual fund options available, it can be challenging to determine which ones are best for beginners. Here are some types of mutual funds that may be well-suited for beginners:

Index funds: Index funds are designed to track a specific stock market index, such as the S&P 500. Because index funds are passively managed, they typically have lower expense ratios than actively managed funds. Additionally, because they are designed to track the overall market, they can offer broad diversification and low volatility. This makes them a great option for beginners who are looking for a simple, low-cost investment option. Target-date funds: Target-date funds are designed to adjust their asset allocation based on the investor's target retirement date. As the target date approaches, the fund automatically shifts its allocation to a more conservative mix of assets. This can be beneficial for beginners who are not familiar with asset allocation and want a simple, hands-off approach to investing. Balanced funds: Balanced funds invest in a mix of stocks and bonds, typically with a focus on capital appreciation and income. Because they invest in both stocks and bonds, they can offer diversification and potentially lower volatility. Additionally, they can be a good option for beginners who want exposure to both asset classes without having to manage two separate investments. Large-cap funds: Large-cap funds invest in companies with large market capitalizations, typically over $10 billion. These companies tend to be more established and stable than smaller companies, which can make them a good option for beginners who want to minimize risk. Additionally, because they invest in large, well-known companies, they can offer a level of familiarity and comfort to new investors. Bond funds: Bond funds invest in fixed income securities such as government and corporate bonds. These funds can offer regular income and potentially lower volatility than stock funds. They can be a good option for beginners who want exposure to fixed income securities but may not have the expertise to invest in individual bonds. It's important to note that these types of mutual funds are not one-size-fits-all and may not be the best option for every investor. It's important for beginners to carefully evaluate their investment goals, risk tolerance, and time horizon before making any investment decisions. Additionally, it's important to consider factors such as fees and expenses, performance history, and risk profile when selecting mutual funds. Consulting with a financial advisor or professional can be a helpful resource in selecting mutual funds that are best for individual investment needs.

Chapter 8
Index Funds

Index funds are a type of mutual fund or exchange-traded fund (ETF) that tracks a specific market index, such as the S&P 500 or the Nasdaq Composite. Unlike actively managed funds, which are managed by fund managers who buy and sell securities based on their own analysis and predictions, index funds are designed to mimic the performance of the underlying index. Index funds are a popular investment option for investors who want to achieve broad market exposure at a low cost. In this chapter, we will explore what index funds are and how to invest in them. What are Index Funds? As mentioned, index funds are designed to track the performance of a specific market index, such as the S&P 500, which is a stock market index that tracks the performance of 500 large-cap U.S. companies. By investing in an index fund, investors can gain exposure to a diversified portfolio of securities that closely matches the performance of the underlying index. Index funds are passively managed, which means that they don't rely on the expertise of a fund manager to make investment decisions. Instead, they are designed to simply follow the performance of the underlying index. This makes them an attractive option for investors who want to achieve broad market exposure without having to pay high fees for active management. Investing in index funds is relatively straightforward, and there are several options for investors to consider. Index mutual funds are a type of mutual fund that tracks a specific market index, such as the S&P 500 or the Dow Jones Industrial Average. Investors can purchase shares of index mutual funds through a brokerage account or a retirement account, such as a 401(k) or an individual retirement account (IRA). When investing in index mutual funds, investors should consider the fund's expense ratio, which is the cost of managing the fund. Index mutual funds generally have lower expense ratios than actively managed funds, but investors should compare the expense ratios of similar funds to ensure that they are getting good value for their investment. Index ETFs are like index mutual funds in that they track a specific market index, but they are traded like stocks on an exchange. This means that investors can buy and sell shares of index ETFs throughout the day, rather than waiting until the end of the trading day to execute trades. Index ETFs can be purchased through a brokerage account, and they often have lower expense ratios than index mutual funds. However, investors should be aware of the bid-ask spread, which is the difference between the price at which an ETF can be bought and the price at which it can be sold. Robo-advisors are automated investment platforms that use algorithms to build and manage investment portfolios for investors. Some robo-advisors, such as Betterment and Wealthfront, offer portfolios that are built using index funds.

Investors can open an account with a robo-advisor and answer a series of questions about their investment goals and risk tolerance. The robo-advisor will then recommend a portfolio of index funds that is tailored to the investor's needs. There are several benefits to investing in index funds, including: Diversification - Index funds offer investors broad market exposure, which can help reduce risk and increase diversification. Low Fees - Index funds generally have lower expense ratios than actively managed funds, which can help investors save money on investment fees over time. Tax Efficiency - Index funds are typically more tax-efficient than actively managed funds because they have lower turnover rates, which means that they generate fewer capital gains distributions. Because index funds simply track the performance of a specific market index, their holdings and performance are transparent. Investors can easily see which securities the fund holds and how the fund is performing relative to the underlying index. Index funds are designed to closely match the performance of the underlying index, which can provide investors with consistent returns over time. Accessibility - Index funds are widely available and can be purchased through a variety of investment platforms, making them accessible to a wide range of investors. While there are many benefits to investing in index funds, it's important for investors to be aware of the potential risks, including: Index funds are subject to market risk, which means that they can experience losses when the underlying index declines. While index funds are designed to closely match the performance of the underlying index, there can be small differences between the fund's performance and the index's performance. This is known as tracking error. Because index funds are designed to track a specific market index, investors may not gain exposure to certain asset classes or sectors that are not included in the index. Some investors may be tempted to invest heavily in index funds that track popular indexes, such as the S&P 500, which can lead to over-concentration in a particular market sector or asset class. Index funds are a popular investment option for investors who want to achieve broad market exposure at a low cost. By investing in index funds, investors can gain exposure to a diversified portfolio of securities that closely matches the performance of the underlying index. There are several ways to invest in index funds, including mutual funds, ETFs, and robo-advisors. When investing in index funds, it's important for investors to consider the fund's expense ratio, performance, and tracking error, as well as the potential risks. Overall, index funds can be an effective tool for building a well-diversified investment portfolio that is appropriate for an investor's needs and risk tolerance. By following these strategies and staying disciplined, investors can achieve their long-term investment goals while managing risk. Index funds can be purchased from a variety of financial institutions, including: Online Brokers: Many online brokers offer a variety of index funds, including mutual funds and exchange-traded funds (ETFs), that can be purchased through their trading platforms. Some popular online brokers include Fidelity, Vanguard, Charles Schwab, and TD Ameritrade. Mutual Fund Companies: Many mutual fund companies, such as Vanguard and Fidelity, offer a variety of index funds that can be purchased directly from their websites or through a financial advisor. Exchange-Traded Funds (ETFs): ETFs can be purchased through a brokerage account, and many online brokers offer commission-free trading on a variety of ETFs. Some popular ETFs that track broad market indexes include the SPDR S&P 500 ETF (SPY), the iShares Core S&P 500 ETF (IVV), and the Vanguard Total Stock Market ETF (VTI). When selecting an index fund, it's important to consider factors such as the fund's expense ratio, performance, and tracking error, as well as the potential risks. It's also important to determine your investment goals and risk tolerance before investing in index funds. A financial advisor or professional can help guide you through the process and help you select the index funds that are appropriate for your needs.

Chapter 9

ETFs

Exchange-traded funds (ETFs) are a type of investment fund that trade on stock exchanges, like individual stocks. They are designed to provide investors with exposure to a wide range of assets, such as stocks, bonds, and commodities, while offering the liquidity and flexibility of a stock investment. In this chapter, we will explore what ETFs are, how they work, and how to invest in them. What are ETFs? ETFs are investment funds that are designed to track the performance of a specific market index or asset class. Like mutual funds, ETFs allow investors to gain exposure to a diversified portfolio of securities. However, ETFs differ from mutual funds in several ways: ETFs trade like stocks: Unlike mutual funds, which are priced at the end of each trading day, ETFs trade throughout the day on stock exchanges, like individual stocks. This means that investors can buy and sell ETF shares at any time during market hours. ETFs are typically passively managed: While some ETFs are actively managed, most are designed to track a specific index or asset class, and they are passively managed. ETFs have lower fees: Because ETFs are typically passively managed, they have lower fees than actively managed funds. Additionally, ETFs do not have front-end or back-end sales charges. Investing in ETFs is relatively straightforward, and there are several ways to do it. Online Brokerages: Most online brokerages offer access to a wide range of ETFs, which can be purchased through their trading platforms. Some popular online brokerages include Fidelity, Vanguard, Charles Schwab, and TD Ameritrade. Robo-Advisors: Some robo-advisors, such as Betterment and Wealthfront, offer portfolios that are built using ETFs. Investors can open an account with a robo-advisor and answer a series of questions about their investment goals and risk tolerance. The robo-advisor will then recommend a portfolio of ETFs that is tailored to the investor's needs. Direct Purchase: Investors can also purchase ETF shares directly from the fund provider. This can be done through the fund provider's website or through a financial advisor. When investing in ETFs, it's important to consider several factors, including - Expense Ratio: The expense ratio is the cost of managing the ETF, and it can have a significant impact on an investor's returns. Investors should look for ETFs with low expense ratios. Liquidity: ETFs trade on stock exchanges, so liquidity can vary depending on the trading volume of the ETF. Investors should look for ETFs with high trading volume and tight bid-ask spreads. Tracking Error: ETFs are designed to track a specific index or asset class, but there can be small differences between the ETF's performance and the index's performance. This is known as tracking error.

Diversification: ETFs can provide investors with exposure to a wide range of assets, but investors should ensure that they are investing in a diversified portfolio of ETFs that is appropriate for their investment goals and risk tolerance. ETFs are a popular investment option for investors who want to gain exposure to a wide range of assets while enjoying the liquidity and flexibility of a stock investment. By investing in ETFs, investors can gain exposure to a diversified portfolio of securities while paying lower fees than actively managed funds. When investing in ETFs, it's important to consider factors such as the expense ratio, liquidity, tracking error, and diversification, as well as your investment goals and risk tolerance. A financial advisor or professional can help guide you through the process and help you select the ETF s that are appropriate for your needs. It's also important to have a long-term investment strategy in mind and to avoid making impulsive decisions based on short-term market fluctuations. One common strategy for investing in ETFs is to build a diversified portfolio that includes a mix of equity, fixed income, and commodity ETFs. This can help to balance risk and returns and provide exposure to a variety of asset classes. Another strategy is to invest in ETFs that track specific market sectors or industries. This can allow investors to gain exposure to areas of the market that they believe will perform well in the future. Regardless of the investment strategy, it's important for investors to regularly monitor their ETF holdings and adjust their portfolio as needed. This can help to ensure that the portfolio remains aligned with the investor's goals and risk tolerance over time. Overall, ETFs can be a valuable tool for building a diversified investment portfolio that is appropriate for an investor's needs and risk tolerance. By considering the factors outlined above and working with a financial advisor or professional, investors can achieve their long-term investment goals while managing risk.

Chapter 10
Security Classifications

Securities are financial instruments that are traded in the financial markets. They represent ownership in a company or a debt obligation that is issued by a company or government entity. Securities are classified into different categories based on their characteristics, such as the type of security, the issuer, and the maturity. There are several types of securities that are commonly traded in the financial markets, including: Stocks: Stocks represent ownership in a company and entitle the holder to a share of the company's profits and assets. Stocks are generally classified as common or preferred, based on the rights and privileges of the holder. Bonds: Bonds are debt securities that are issued by companies or government entities. They represent a loan from the holder to the issuer and pay a fixed rate of interest over a specified period. Bonds are classified based on the issuer, the interest rate, and the maturity. Mutual Funds: Mutual funds are investment vehicles that pool the money of multiple investors to purchase a diversified portfolio of stocks, bonds, and other securities. Mutual funds are classified based on the type of assets they hold, such as stocks, bonds, or a combination of both. Exchange-Traded Funds (ETFs): ETFs are like mutual funds, but they are traded on stock exchanges like individual stocks. ETFs are classified based on the type of assets they hold, such as stocks, bonds, or commodities. Options: Options are contracts that give the holder the right, but not the obligation, to buy or sell an underlying asset at a specified price within a specified period. Options are classified based on the type of option, the underlying asset, and the expiration date. Futures: Futures are contracts that require the holder to buy or sell an underlying asset at a specified price at a specified date in the future. Futures are commonly traded in commodities, such as oil, gold, and wheat, but they can also be traded in financial assets, such as currencies and stock indexes. In addition to these types of securities, there are also derivative securities, which are financial instruments that derive their value from an underlying asset or security. Derivative securities include options, futures, and swaps. Securities can also be classified based on the issuer, such as government securities or corporate securities. Government securities are issued by government entities, such as the U.S. Treasury, and are generally considered to be low-risk investments. Corporate securities are issued by companies and can range from low-risk to high-risk investments, depending on the creditworthiness of the issuer. Securities can also be classified based on their maturity, such as short-term or long-term securities. Short-term securities have a maturity of less than one year, while long-term securities have a maturity of more than one year.

Finally, securities can be classified based on their market capitalization, which is the total value of all outstanding shares of a company's stock. Large-cap stocks have a market capitalization of more than $10 billion, while mid-cap stocks have a market capitalization of between $2 billion and $10 billion. Small-cap stocks have a market capitalization of less than $2 billion. Securities are classified into different categories based on their characteristics, such as the type of security, the issuer, the maturity, and the market capitalization. Understanding these classifications can help investors make informed decisions about their investments and build a diversified portfolio that is appropriate for their needs and risk tolerance.

Chapter 11
Business Driven Investing

Business-driven investing is an investment approach that focuses on the fundamental performance of a company and its ability to generate profits and growth. This approach considers the underlying business model, management team, industry dynamics, and competitive landscape of a company to identify investment opportunities with the potential for long-term success. Business-driven investing differs from other investment approaches, such as technical analysis or momentum investing, which focus on short-term market trends and fluctuations. Instead, business-driven investing is based on the belief that the long-term success of a company is driven by its ability to generate sustained earnings growth and competitive advantage. The key principles of business-driven investing include -Focus on the underlying business: Business-driven investors focus on the fundamental performance of a company, rather than short-term market trends or fluctuations. They analyze a company's financial statements, management team, industry dynamics, and competitive landscape to identify investment opportunities with the potential for long-term success. Invest for the long-term: Business-driven investors have a long-term investment horizon and are willing to hold onto their investments for several years, if not decades. They understand that the underlying business of a company is the primary driver of long-term returns, and that short-term fluctuations are often noise. Diversify: Business-driven investors understand the importance of diversification and build portfolios that are diversified across different industries, geographies, and asset classes. By diversifying their portfolios, they can reduce their exposure to specific risks and take advantage of a broad range of investment opportunities. Active management: Business-driven investors actively manage their portfolios and are constantly looking for new investment opportunities. They are not afraid to sell their holdings if they believe that the underlying business is deteriorating or if the valuation is no longer attractive. Business-driven investing can be applied to a variety of asset classes, including stocks, bonds, and alternative investments. When investing in stocks, business-driven investors look for companies with a sustainable competitive advantage, a strong management team, and a track record of consistent earnings growth. They also pay attention to valuations, and will only invest in companies that they believe are undervalued. When investing in bonds, business-driven investors focus on the creditworthiness of the issuer and the underlying fundamentals of the business. They also pay attention to the yield curve and the overall economic environment to identify opportunities for long-term returns. In alternative investments, such as private equity or real estate, business-driven investors focus on the underlying business model and the potential for long-term growth. They also pay attention to the management team, the competitive landscape, and the regulatory environment to identify opportunities for long-term success. Business-driven investing is an investment approach that focuses on the underlying business of a company and its ability to generate sustained earnings growth and competitive advantage. This approach considers the fundamentals of the business, the management team, and the competitive landscape to identify opportunities for long-term success. By applying the principles of business-driven investing, investors can build diversified portfolios that are well-positioned to generate long-term returns. There are many companies that could be considered as examples of business-driven investing. Here are a few: Amazon (AMZN): Amazon is a company that has disrupted multiple industries and has become a household name around the world. The company's business model is focused on e-commerce, cloud computing, and digital media. Amazon has a strong management team, led by founder Jeff Bezos, and a track record of consistent earnings growth. Despite its success, Amazon continues to invest heavily in new businesses and technologies, which could provide additional growth opportunities in the future. Microsoft (MSFT): Microsoft is a technology company that is focused on software, hardware, and services. The company has a strong competitive position in the enterprise market, with its Windows operating system and Office productivity suite. Microsoft has also been successful in the cloud computing market, with its Azure platform. The company has a strong management team, led by CEO Satya Nadella, and has consistently delivered earnings growth and dividends to shareholders. Alphabet (GOOGL): Alphabet is the parent company of Google, which is the dominant player in the online search and advertising market. Alphabet also has a significant presence in the cloud computing, mobile operating system, and smart home markets. The company has a strong management team, led by CEO Sundar Pichai, and has consistently delivered earnings growth and stock price appreciation to shareholders. Johnson & Johnson (JNJ): Johnson & Johnson is a healthcare company that operates in the pharmaceutical, medical device, and consumer health markets. The company has a diversified business model and a strong competitive position in many of its markets. Johnson & Johnson has a long history of delivering consistent earnings growth and dividends to shareholders, and has a strong management team that is focused on innovation and long-term growth. Visa (V): Visa is a payment technology company that operates in the global payments market. The company has a strong competitive position, with a dominant market share in the credit and debit card markets. Visa has a strong management team, led by CEO Alfred Kelly Jr., and has consistently delivered earnings growth and stock price appreciation to shareholders. These are just a few examples of companies that could be considered as business-driven investments. It's important to conduct thorough research and analysis before making any investment decisions, and to ensure that your investments align with your investment goals and risk tolerance.

Chapter 12
Security Analysis

Security analysis is a process of evaluating securities, such as stocks, bonds, and other financial instruments, to determine their intrinsic value and make investment decisions. The goal of security analysis is to identify securities that are trading below their intrinsic value, and to avoid those that are overvalued. In modern sense, security analysis has become more complex due to the rise of new technologies, financial instruments, and market dynamics. In today's market, security analysis often involves a combination of quantitative and qualitative analysis, as well as an understanding of market trends and global economic forces. Quantitative analysis involves using mathematical models and statistical techniques to analyze financial data, such as revenue, earnings, and cash flows, to identify trends and patterns. This can involve using financial ratios, such as price-to-earnings (P/E) ratio or earnings-per-share (EPS), to compare the financial performance of different companies. Qualitative analysis involves evaluating non-financial factors, such as a company's management team, competitive position, industry dynamics, and macroeconomic trends. This can involve conducting interviews with management, analyzing industry reports, and monitoring news and social media for relevant information. In addition to these traditional forms of security analysis, modern security analysis has also been influenced by the rise of new technologies, such as artificial intelligence (AI) and machine learning. These technologies can be used to analyze large volumes of data and identify trends and patterns that may be difficult to identify through traditional analysis methods. Another important aspect of modern security analysis is the use of big data and data analytics. By collecting and analyzing vast amounts of data, investors can gain insights into market trends, consumer behavior, and other key factors that may impact the performance of securities. Finally, modern security analysis also requires an understanding of global economic forces and market dynamics. This can involve monitoring global news and events, such as changes in interest rates, political instability, or global economic trends, and how they may impact the performance of securities. Security analysis in modern sense is a complex and multifaceted process that requires a combination of quantitative and qualitative analysis, as well as an understanding of market trends, global economic forces, and new technologies. By conducting thorough security analysis, investors can identify undervalued securities and make informed investment decisions that can lead to long-term success. Security analysis is a process of evaluating securities, such as stocks, bonds, and other financial instruments, to determine their intrinsic value and make investment decisions. The process of security analysis is typically broken down into three major parts: Fundamental Analysis: Fundamental analysis is the process of evaluating the financial health and performance of a company to determine its intrinsic value. This involves analyzing a company's financial statements, management team, competitive position, and industry dynamics to gain insight into its prospects. The main objective of fundamental analysis is to determine whether a company is undervalued or overvalued by the market. This involves analyzing financial ratios, such as the price-to-earnings (P/E) ratio, earnings-per-share (EPS), and return-on-equity (ROE), to assess the company's financial performance relative to its peers. Fundamental analysis also involves evaluating the company's competitive position in the market, including its market share, growth prospects, and management team. This can involve analyzing industry reports, attending industry conferences, and conducting interviews with company management. Technical Analysis: Technical analysis is the process of evaluating securities based on past price and volume data to identify trends and patterns. This involves analyzing charts and other technical indicators to gain insight into market trends and to identify potential trading opportunities.

The main objective of technical analysis is to identify patterns in market data that can be used to predict future price movements. This can involve analyzing charts and other technical indicators, such as moving averages, relative strength indicators (RSI), and trend lines. Technical analysis also involves monitoring market sentiment, such as investor sentiment and market trends, in order to identify potential trading opportunities. Quantitative Analysis: Quantitative analysis is the process of evaluating securities based on mathematical models and statistical techniques to identify trends and patterns. This involves analyzing financial data, such as revenue, earnings, and cash flows, to identify trends and patterns. The main objective of quantitative analysis is to identify undervalued securities by comparing the financial performance of different companies. This can involve using financial ratios, such as the price-to-earnings (P/E) ratio, earnings-per-share (EPS), and return-on-equity (ROE), to compare the financial performance of different companies. Quantitative analysis also involves using complex mathematical models and statistical techniques, such as regression analysis and Monte Carlo simulation, to identify trends and patterns that may be difficult to identify through traditional analysis methods. The three major parts of security analysis are fundamental analysis, technical analysis, and quantitative analysis. By using a combination of these methods, investors can gain insight into the financial health and performance of a company, identify trends and patterns in market data, and make informed investment decisions that can lead to long-term success. Monte Carlo simulation is a statistical technique that is used to model complex systems and processes. It is named after the famous Monte Carlo Casino in Monaco, where chance and probability play a significant role. Monte Carlo simulation is widely used in finance, engineering, science, and other fields to simulate complex systems and generate data for analysis. Monte Carlo simulation involves generating many random samples, based on probability distributions that are representative of the system being modeled. These samples are then used to estimate the probability of different outcomes and to simulate the behavior of the system under different conditions. For example, Monte Carlo simulation can be used to estimate the probability of a stock price reaching a certain level in the future, based on historical data and the assumptions about future market conditions. By generating a large number of random simulations, analysts can estimate the probability of different outcomes, such as the stock price exceeding a certain level, and use this information to make informed investment decisions. The process of Monte Carlo simulation involves several steps: Define the Problem: The first step in Monte Carlo simulation is to define the problem being modeled and the variables that will be used. This involves identifying the key variables and assumptions that will be used in the simulation. Define the Probability Distributions: Once the variables have been identified, the next step is to define the probability distributions that will be used to generate the random samples. This involves selecting the appropriate probability distribution for each variable, such as a normal distribution or a lognormal distribution. Generate the Random Samples: Once the probability distributions have been defined, the next step is to generate the random samples. This involves using a computer program to generate many random samples, based on the probability distributions defined in step two. Analyze the Results: Once the random samples have been generated, the next step is to analyze the results. This involves using statistical techniques to estimate the probability of different outcomes and to identify patterns and trends in the data. Monte Carlo simulation has several advantages, including the ability to model complex systems and to generate data that can be used to make informed decisions. It is also a flexible technique that can be used to model a wide range of systems, including financial models, engineering models, and scientific models. However, Monte Carlo simulation also has some limitations. One of the main limitations is that it relies on the assumptions and probability distributions that are used to generate the random samples. If these assumptions are incorrect or the probability distributions are not representative of the system being modeled, the results of the simulation may be inaccurate or unreliable. Additionally, Monte Carlo simulation can be computationally intensive, requiring significant computing power to generate many random samples. Monte Carlo simulation is a powerful statistical technique that can be used to model complex systems and to generate data for analysis. It is widely used in finance, engineering, science, and other fields to simulate complex systems and to generate data that can be used to make informed decisions. While Monte Carlo simulation has some limitations, it remains a valuable tool for analyzing complex systems and generating data for decision-making.

Chapter 13
Preferred Stock Investments

Preferred stocks are a type of security that offers a fixed dividend payment to investors, typically with priority over common stockholders. They are often seen as a hybrid between stocks and bonds, as they offer a steady income stream but also the potential for capital appreciation. As with any investment, selecting preferred stocks requires a thorough understanding of the underlying fundamentals and market conditions. Here are some techniques for selecting preferred stocks for investment: Research the Company: The first step in selecting preferred stocks for investment is to research the underlying company. This includes analyzing the company's financial statements, management team, competitive position, and industry dynamics. It is important to look for companies with a strong track record of profitability and a solid balance sheet. Assess the Yield: The yield on a preferred stock is the dividend payment as a percentage of the stock price. A higher yield can indicate a higher degree of risk, so it is important to consider the company's financial health and the sustainability of the dividend payment. It is also important to compare the yield of the preferred stock to other similar securities to determine if it is competitive. Examine the Credit Rating: Credit ratings can provide an indication of the underlying company's financial strength and ability to make dividend payments. It is important to look for companies with a strong credit rating, as this can indicate a lower degree of risk. Consider the Call Provisions: Many preferred stocks have call provisions, which allow the issuer to redeem the stock at a certain price after a specified period. It is important to consider the call provisions when selecting preferred stocks, as they can impact the potential return on investment. Evaluate the Market Conditions: The broader market conditions can impact the performance of preferred stocks. It is important to consider factors such as interest rates, inflation, and market volatility when selecting preferred stocks for investment. Diversify: Diversification is key to managing risk in any investment portfolio. It is important to consider investing in a variety of preferred stocks, as well as other securities such as bonds and common stocks, to spread out risk and potentially maximize returns. Consult with a Financial Advisor: It can be helpful to consult with a financial advisor when selecting preferred stocks for investment. A financial advisor can provide insight into market conditions and help identify preferred stocks that align with an investor's goals and risk tolerance. Selecting preferred stocks for investment requires a thorough understanding of the underlying company and market conditions. By researching the company, assessing the yield, examining the credit rating, considering the call provisions, evaluating the market conditions, diversifying, and consulting with a financial advisor, investors can potentially identify preferred stocks that offer a steady income stream and potential for capital appreciation. Preferred stocks are issued by many different companies across a variety of industries. Here are some examples of companies that issue preferred stocks: Bank of America: Bank of America issues several series of preferred stocks, including Series W, Series V, and Series L. These preferred stocks offer a fixed dividend payment and are typically traded on major stock exchanges. JPMorgan Chase: JPMorgan Chase issues several series of preferred stocks, including Series V and Series T. These preferred stocks offer a fixed dividend payment and are typically traded on major stock exchanges. Ford: Ford issues several series of preferred stocks, including Series B and Series C. These preferred stocks offer a fixed dividend payment and are typically traded on major stock exchanges. Verizon: Verizon issues several series of preferred stocks, including Series C, Series D, and Series E. These preferred stocks offer a fixed dividend payment and are typically traded on major stock exchanges. Coca-Cola: Coca-Cola issues several series of preferred stocks, including Series A, Series B, and Series C. These preferred stocks offer a fixed dividend payment and are typically traded on major stock exchanges. AT&T: AT&T issues several series of preferred stocks, including Series A, Series C, and Series D. These preferred stocks offer a fixed dividend payment and are typically traded on major stock exchanges. Pfizer: Pfizer issues several series of preferred stocks, including Series D and Series E. These preferred stocks offer a fixed dividend payment and are typically traded on major stock exchanges. Preferred stocks are issued by many different companies across a variety of industries. These stocks offer a fixed dividend payment and are typically traded on major stock exchanges. By researching the underlying company and market conditions, investors can potentially identify preferred stocks that align with their investment goals and risk tolerance. Preferred stock protective provisions are features that are included in preferred stock agreements to protect the rights and interests of the investors who hold these securities. These provisions are typically negotiated between the issuer of the preferred stock and the investor and are designed to address a variety of concerns related to the issuance and management of preferred stock. Here are some examples of common preferred stock protective provisions: Dividend Preference: A dividend preference provision gives preferred stockholders priority over common stockholders when it comes to receiving dividend payments. This means that if the company must cut its dividend payments, the preferred stockholders will receive their payments before the common stockholders. Conversion Rights: Conversion rights give the preferred stockholders the right to convert their shares into common stock at a predetermined ratio. This provision can be beneficial to investors if the company's common stock experiences significant price appreciation. Call Protection: Call protection provisions limit the ability of the issuer to redeem the preferred stock before a certain date. This can provide investors with more stability and predictability when it comes to receiving dividend payments. Liquidation Preference: Liquidation preference provisions give preferred stockholders priority over common stockholders when it comes to receiving proceeds from the sale of the company or in the event of bankruptcy. This means that if the company is liquidated, the preferred stockholders will receive their payments before the common stockholders. Voting Rights: Some preferred stock agreements include voting rights for preferred stockholders. These provisions may give preferred stockholders the right to vote on certain issues related to the company, such as changes to the company's capital structure. Protective Covenants: Protective covenants are provisions that are designed to protect the interests of the preferred stockholders in the event of certain events, such as a merger or acquisition. These provisions may include restrictions on the ability of the company to issue additional preferred stock or to make certain changes to its business operations. Preferred stock protective provisions are an important consideration for investors who are considering investing in these securities. These provisions can provide investors with added protection and security, while also addressing concerns related to the issuance and management of preferred stock. By understanding the different types of preferred stock protective provisions, investors can make informed decisions about the preferred stocks they choose to invest in.

Chapter 14
Supervision of Investment Holdings

Supervision of investment holdings refers to the process of overseeing and monitoring an investor's portfolio of securities, including stocks, bonds, and other investment vehicles. This process is important to ensure that the portfolio remains aligned with the investor's goals and risk tolerance, and to identify any potential issues or risks that may arise. Here are some key steps involved in the supervision of investment holdings: Regular Monitoring: It is important to regularly monitor the investor's portfolio to ensure that it remains aligned with their goals and risk tolerance. This includes tracking the performance of individual securities and the portfolio as a whole and making adjustments as necessary to maintain the desired level of diversification and risk exposure. Risk Management: Risk management is an important component of the supervision of investment holdings. This involves identifying and assessing the risks associated with individual securities and the portfolio as a whole and implementing strategies to mitigate these risks. For example, an investor may choose to diversify their portfolio across different sectors or asset classes to reduce the risk of concentration in any one area. Rebalancing: Rebalancing involves periodically adjusting the portfolio to maintain the desired level of diversification and risk exposure. This may involve selling securities that have become overvalued or overrepresented in the portfolio, and reinvesting the proceeds in other securities that are more aligned with the investor's goals and risk tolerance. Reporting: It is important to provide regular reporting on the performance of the portfolio and the individual securities held within it. This can help the investor to better understand how their portfolio is performing, and to identify any potential issues or risks that may arise. Consultation: Consulting with a financial advisor or professional can be helpful in the supervision of investment holdings. A financial advisor can provide insight into market conditions and help identify potential risks and opportunities, as well as provide guidance on strategies for managing risk and achieving investment goals. The supervision of investment holdings is an important process for ensuring that an investor's portfolio remains aligned with their goals and risk tolerance, and to identify any potential issues or risks that may arise. By regularly monitoring the portfolio, managing risk, rebalancing, providing regular reporting, and consulting with a financial advisor or professional, investors can potentially maximize returns and achieve their investment objectives. Balancing risk in a stock portfolio is an important aspect of investing. A well-balanced portfolio should include a mix of stocks with different levels of risk, in order to achieve a balance between potential returns and potential losses. Here are some strategies for balancing risk in a stock portfolio: Diversification: Diversification is key to balancing risk in a stock portfolio. This involves investing in a mix of different stocks across different industries and sectors, to spread out risk and potentially maximize returns. By diversifying your portfolio, you can reduce the impact of any one stock or sector on your overall portfolio performance. Asset Allocation: Asset allocation refers to the percentage of your portfolio that is invested in different asset classes, such as stocks, bonds, and cash. By allocating your portfolio across different asset classes, you can balance risk and potential returns. For example, if you are a conservative investor, you may choose to allocate a higher percentage of your portfolio to bonds and cash, and a lower percentage to stocks. Risk Tolerance: Your risk tolerance is a measure of your willingness and ability to take on risk in your portfolio. When balancing risk in a stock portfolio, it is important to consider your risk tolerance and choose stocks that align with your comfort level. For example, if you have a low risk tolerance, you may choose to invest in more conservative, stable stocks that offer lower potential returns but also lower potential losses. Fundamental Analysis: Fundamental analysis involves analyzing the underlying financial performance of a company, including factors such as revenue growth, earnings, and debt levels. By conducting fundamental analysis, you can gain insight into the potential risks and rewards of investing in a particular stock. Technical Analysis: Technical analysis involves analyzing the price and volume movements of a stock to identify trends and patterns. By using technical analysis, you can gain insight into the potential risks and rewards of investing in a particular stock and make more informed decisions about when to buy or sell. Stop Loss Orders: A stop loss order is a type of order that automatically sells a stock if it falls below a certain price. By using stop loss orders, you can limit potential losses in your portfolio and balance risk. Balancing risk in a stock portfolio is an important aspect of investing. By diversifying your portfolio, allocating your assets appropriately, considering your risk tolerance, conducting fundamental and technical analysis, and using stop loss orders, you can potentially maximize returns and minimize losses. It is important to regularly review and rebalance your portfolio to ensure that it remains aligned with your investment goals and risk tolerance.

Chapter 15
Dividend Stocks

Dividend stocks are stocks that pay out a portion of their earnings to shareholders in the form of regular dividends. These stocks are popular with investors seeking steady income streams and potentially lower levels of risk. In this chapter, we will cover some key aspects of dividend stocks, including their benefits, risks, and how to evaluate them as potential investments. Benefits of Dividend Stocks: Income Generation: Dividend stocks can provide a reliable source of income for investors. By reinvesting dividends or using them as a source of income, investors can potentially generate a steady stream of cash flow. Lower Risk: Dividend stocks are often considered less risky than non-dividend paying stocks. This is because companies that pay dividends tend to be more established and financially stable and are typically generating consistent profits. Long-Term Growth: Companies that pay dividends tend to be well-established and have a track record of consistent earnings. This can be a sign of long-term growth potential for the company and may lead to appreciation in the stock price over time. Risks of Dividend Stocks: Market Risk: Like all stocks, dividend stocks are subject to market risk. This means that their value can fluctuate based on overall market conditions and investor sentiment. Interest Rate Risk: Dividend stocks can be affected by changes in interest rates. When interest rates rise, dividend stocks may become less attractive to investors, as they may prefer to invest in fixed income securities that offer higher returns. Dividend Risk: Dividend payments are not guaranteed and can be reduced or eliminated by the company at any time. This can occur if the company experiences financial difficulties, if it decides to reinvest earnings into the business instead of paying dividends, or if it chooses to repurchase shares instead of paying dividends. Evaluating Dividend Stocks: When evaluating dividend stocks, there are several factors to consider, including: Dividend Yield: The dividend yield is the percentage of the stock price that is paid out in dividends annually. A higher yield may indicate a more attractive investment, but it is important to consider the sustainability of the dividend payout. Payout Ratio: The payout ratio is the percentage of earnings that are paid out in dividends. A high payout ratio may indicate that the company is paying out too much of its earnings and may not be sustainable in the long run. Dividend Growth: The growth rate of the dividend over time can be an important factor to consider. Companies that consistently increase their dividends may indicate a commitment to returning value to shareholders. Financial Stability: It is important to evaluate the financial stability of the company paying the dividend. This includes looking at factors such as debt levels, cash flow, and earnings growth. Examples of Dividend Stocks: Johnson & Johnson (JNJ): Johnson & Johnson is a healthcare company that has consistently paid dividends for over 50 years. It has a dividend yield of around 2.5% and a strong financial position. Procter & Gamble (PG): Procter & Gamble is a consumer goods company that has been paying dividends for over 120 years. It has a dividend yield of around 2.5% and a history of increasing its dividend payout over time. Verizon Communications (VZ): Verizon is a telecommunications company that has paid dividends for over 30 years. It has a dividend yield of around 4.5% and a strong financial position. Dividend stocks can provide investors with a reliable source of income and potentially lower levels of risk. However, it is important to consider the potential risks and evaluate dividend stocks based on factors such as dividend yield, payout ratio, dividend growth, and financial stability. By carefully evaluating dividend stocks, investors can potentially identify attractive investments that align with their investment goals and risk tolerance. It is important to note that dividend stocks are just one type of investment and should be evaluated in the context of an overall investment portfolio. Diversification across asset classes, sectors, and geographies is important for managing risk and achieving long-term investment goals. When investing in dividend stocks, it is also important to consider the tax implications of dividend income. Dividends are typically taxed at a lower rate than other types of investment income, but it is important to consult with a tax advisor to fully understand the tax implications of dividend investing. Overall, dividend stocks can be an attractive investment option for investors seeking reliable income streams and potentially lower levels of risk. By carefully evaluating dividend stocks based on factors such as dividend yield, payout ratio, dividend growth, and financial stability, investors can potentially identify attractive investments that align with their investment goals and risk tolerance. As with all investments, it is important to conduct thorough research and seek the advice of a financial professional before making any investment decisions. the highest paying dividend stock is New Residential Investment Corp (NRZ), which currently has a dividend yield of around 10%. However, it is important to note that dividend yield is not the only factor to consider when evaluating stocks as potential investments. Here are some other high dividends yielding stock: AT&T Inc. (T): AT&T is a telecommunications company that currently has a dividend yield of around 7.3%. The company has a long history of paying dividends and has consistently increased its dividend payout over time. Energy Transfer LP (ET): Energy Transfer is a midstream energy company that currently has a dividend yield of around 7%. The company operates pipelines and other energy infrastructure and has a relatively stable business model. Verizon Communications Inc. (VZ): Verizon is a telecommunications company that currently has a dividend yield of around 4.5%. The company has a strong financial position and a history of paying and increasing its dividend payout. Iron Mountain Inc. (IRM): Iron Mountain is a data storage and management company that currently has a dividend yield of around 4.2%. The company has a relatively stable business model and a history of consistent dividend payments. Altria Group Inc. (MO): Altria Group is a tobacco company that currently has a dividend yield of around 7.6%. The company has a long history of paying dividends, but it is important to note that the tobacco industry is subject to regulatory and litigation risks. It is important to note that high dividend yields can sometimes be a warning sign of potential financial trouble for a company. Investors should always conduct thorough research and consider factors such as financial stability, growth potential, and industry trends when evaluating dividend-paying stocks as potential investments. Additionally, it is important to consider the tax implications of dividend income when investing in dividend-paying stocks. Dividends are typically taxed at a lower rate than other types of investment income, but it is important to consult with a tax advisor to fully understand the tax implications of dividend investing. Overall, high dividend-paying stocks can be an attractive investment option for investors seeking reliable income streams. However, it is important to carefully evaluate potential investments based on a variety of factors and consider the potential risks and tax implications of dividend investing. Buying a stock for dividend income can be a good strategy for some investors, particularly those seeking a reliable source of income or those looking to diversify their investment portfolio. However, there are some factors to consider before making an investment solely based on a company's dividend payment. One important factor to consider is the financial stability of the company paying the dividend. A company with a history of consistent earnings and a strong balance sheet is more likely to continue paying dividends in the future. Conversely, a company with a weak financial position may be forced to cut or eliminate its dividend payments. Another factor to consider is the sustainability of the dividend payment. A company with a high dividend yield may seem attractive, but it is important to evaluate whether the dividend payment is sustainable in the long run. A high dividend payout ratio (the percentage of earnings paid out as dividends) may indicate that the company is paying out too much of its earnings and may not be able to sustain the dividend payment in the future. It is also important to consider the potential risks associated with investing in dividend-paying stocks. Like all stocks, dividend-paying stocks are subject to market risk and their value can fluctuate based on overall market conditions and investor sentiment. Additionally, dividend payments are not guaranteed and can be reduced or eliminated by the company at any time. Buying a stock for dividend income can be a good strategy for some investors, but it is important to carefully evaluate potential investments based on factors such as financial stability, sustainability of the dividend payment, and potential risks associated with investing in dividend-paying stocks. As with all investments, it is important to conduct thorough research and seek the advice of a financial professional before making any investment decisions. Dividends are a portion of a company's profits that are paid out to shareholders on a regular basis. They can provide a reliable source of income for investors seeking regular cash flow from their investments. However, not all companies pay dividends, and dividend payments can be reduced or eliminated if the company's financial performance declines. Additionally, the price of the stock can still fluctuate based on market conditions and other factors. Stock ownership, on the other hand, represents a share of ownership in a company. This ownership can provide long-term capital appreciation as the company's value increases over time. However, there is no guarantee of capital appreciation and the stock price can also decline. In general, it is important to have a diversified investment portfolio that includes a mix of stocks, bonds, and other assets that align with your investment goals and risk tolerance. Dividend-paying stocks can be a valuable component of a diversified portfolio for investors seeking reliable income streams, but it is important to evaluate potential investments based on factors such as financial stability, sustainability of the dividend payment, and potential risks associated with investing in dividend-paying stocks. Ultimately, whether dividends or stocks are better for a particular investor depends on individual circumstances and investment goals. It is important to conduct thorough research and seek the advice of a financial professional before making any investment decisions. As a beginner investor, investing in dividend stocks can be a good strategy for building a portfolio with potential for long-term growth and income. However, it is important to approach dividend investing with a clear understanding of the potential risks and rewards. One benefit of investing in dividend stocks is the potential for reliable income streams. Dividend-paying companies have a track record of returning a portion of their profits to shareholders, which can provide a consistent source of income. Additionally, dividend stocks can potentially provide a degree of stability in an investor's portfolio, as dividend payments can help offset declines in the stock price. However, it is important to keep in mind that dividend payments are not guaranteed and can be reduced or eliminated by the company at any time. Additionally, investing in individual stocks requires careful research and analysis to ensure that the investment aligns with an investor's goals and risk tolerance. For beginner investors, it may be helpful to start by investing in dividend-oriented mutual funds or exchange-traded funds (ETFs), which offer exposure to a diversified portfolio of dividend-paying stocks. This can provide exposure to dividend-paying companies across multiple industries and sectors, while also providing a degree of diversification and potentially lower risk than investing in individual stocks. Overall, investing in dividend stocks can be a valuable strategy for beginner investors seeking long-term growth and income, but it is important to conduct thorough research, diversify investments, and seek the advice of a financial professional before making any investment decisions. Dividend stocks can be an attractive investment option for investors seeking income and stability in their portfolio. Here are some of the factors to consider when selecting a good dividend stock: Dividend yield: The dividend yield is the annual dividend payment divided by the current stock price. A high dividend yield can indicate that the company is generating strong cash flows and is committed to returning value to shareholders. However, it is important to note that a high yield can also indicate a risky investment or a company in financial distress, so investors should consider other factors as well. Dividend history: It is important to evaluate a company's dividend history before investing in a dividend stock. Look for companies with a consistent track record of paying dividends over time, as this can be a sign of financial stability and a commitment to returning value to shareholders. Payout ratio: The payout ratio is the percentage of earnings that is paid out as dividends. A high payout ratio can indicate that the company is returning a significant portion of its earnings to shareholders, but it can also indicate that the company is not reinvesting enough in its business for future growth. A low payout ratio, on the other hand, can indicate that the company is reinvesting more of its earnings in its business. Financial health: It is important to evaluate a company's financial health before investing in a dividend stock. Look for companies with strong balance sheets, stable earnings growth, and a manageable debt load. A company with a strong financial position is more likely to be able to sustain its dividend payments over time. Industry trends: Consider the trends in the industry that the company operates in. If the industry is in decline or facing significant challenges, it may be more difficult for the company to sustain its dividend payments. On the other hand, if the industry is growing and has favorable long-term prospects, the company may be better positioned to continue paying dividends over time. Management track record: Evaluate the track record of the company's management team in terms of financial performance, capital allocation, and dividend policies. Look for a management team that has a proven track record of making smart investments, returning value to shareholders, and navigating through challenging market conditions. Valuation: Consider the valuation of the company's stock before investing in a dividend stock. Look for companies that are trading at reasonable valuations relative to their earnings and cash flows. A stock that is trading at a high valuation may be more vulnerable to a correction or downturn in the market. By considering these factors, investors can potentially identify good dividend stocks that align with their investment goals and risk tolerance. However, it is important to note that investing in dividend stocks carries risks and investors should carefully evaluate their individual circumstances and consult with a financial advisor before making any investment decisions.

Chapter 16
The Secret

Warren Buffett's success in investing is attributed to several key factors, including his adherence to value investing principles, his focus on long-term thinking, and his ability to identify and invest in high-quality companies at reasonable prices. Here are some of the key secrets to Warren Buffett's success in investing: Value investing principles: Warren Buffett's investment strategy is based on the principles of value investing, which were pioneered by his mentor Benjamin Graham. Value investing involves looking for companies that are trading at a discount to their intrinsic value, or the true value of the company's assets and earnings potential. By buying companies at a discount, investors can potentially benefit from price appreciation as the market recognizes the true value of the company. Long-term thinking: Warren Buffett is known for his long-term investment horizon, often holding onto stocks for years or even decades. This approach allows him to benefit from the power of compounding, as his investments grow over time. Additionally, by focusing on the long-term prospects of a company, Buffett can tune out short-term fluctuations in stock price and make investment decisions based on the company's underlying fundamentals. Focus on quality companies: Buffett is known for investing in high-quality companies with strong financials, a competitive advantage, and a durable business model. He looks for companies with a strong brand, a long history of profitability, and a management team with a proven track record of success. By investing in high-quality companies, Buffett can reduce his risk and benefit from the potential for long-term growth. Patience and discipline: Buffett are known for his patience and discipline in investing. He does not make impulsive investment decisions, instead taking his time to conduct thorough research and analysis before deciding. Additionally, he is willing to wait for the right opportunity to come along, even if it means sitting on the sidelines for long periods of time. Continuous learning: Despite his success, Warren Buffett is known for his commitment to continuous learning. He reads extensively, attends conferences and shareholder meetings, and seeks out advice and mentorship from other successful investors. By continuously learning and adapting his approach to investing, Buffett can stay ahead of the curve and identify new investment opportunities. Humility and integrity: Buffett are known for his humility and integrity, both in his personal life and in his investing approach. He is willing to admit when he makes mistakes and learn from them, and he always acts with honesty and transparency in his business dealings. This reputation for integrity has helped him build strong relationships with investors, companies, and the wider business community. In summary, Warren Buffett's success in investing is due to a combination of factors, including his adherence to value investing principles, his long-term focus, his ability to identify high-quality companies, his patience and discipline, his commitment to continuous learning, and his reputation for humility and integrity. By following these principles, beginner investors may be able to learn from Buffett's success and apply them to their own investing approach. Patience and discipline are two of the most important qualities for successful stock investing. In a world where news and information travel quickly, it can be easy to make impulsive decisions based on short-term market fluctuations. However, the most successful investors understand the value of patience and discipline in achieving long-term investment goals. Patience in stock investing involves taking a long-term view and being willing to wait for the right investment opportunities to come along. It means not being swayed by short-term market trends or emotional reactions to news and events. Instead, patient investors take the time to research and analyze potential investments, weighing the risks and rewards before deciding. Discipline in stock investing involves sticking to a predetermined investment strategy, even in the face of market volatility or unexpected events. It means having a clear understanding of one's investment goals and risk tolerance and making investment decisions based on those factors rather than being swayed by market trends or the latest hot stock tip. Together, patience and discipline can help investors avoid costly mistakes and achieve long-term investment success. Here are some of the ways that these qualities can benefit stock investors: Avoiding emotional reactions: When the market experiences volatility or unexpected events occur, it can be tempting to make impulsive investment decisions based on emotions rather than logic. However, patient, and disciplined investors can maintain a clear-headed perspective and avoid making decisions based on fear or anxiety. Staying focused on long-term goals: Investing in the stock market is a long-term endeavor, and patient and disciplined investors understand that short-term market fluctuations are a normal part of the process. By maintaining a long-term perspective and sticking to their investment strategy, they can stay focused on their goals and avoid getting sidetracked by short-term distractions. Conducting thorough research and analysis: Patience and discipline allow investors to take the time to conduct thorough research and analysis before making an investment decision. This includes analyzing a company's financials, competitive landscape, and growth prospects, as well as evaluating market trends and potential risks. By taking the time to conduct this analysis, investors can make more informed investment decisions and potentially achieve better long-term returns. Avoiding herd mentality: In the stock market, there is often a tendency for investors to follow the crowd and chase after the latest hot stock or trend. However, patient, and disciplined investors can resist this herd mentality and make investment decisions based on their own analysis and judgment, rather than simply following the crowd. In summary, patience and discipline are essential qualities for successful stock investing. By taking a long-term view, staying focused on investment goals, conducting thorough research and analysis, and avoiding herd mentality, investors can potentially achieve better long-term returns and avoid costly mistakes. Warren Buffett, one of the most successful investors of all time, has long been a proponent of index funds as a valuable tool for building wealth. Here are some of the reasons why Buffett likes index funds: Low costs: Buffett has famously emphasized the importance of keeping investment costs low, and index funds are one of the most cost-effective investment options available. Since index funds are designed to track a specific market index, they require less management and research than actively managed funds, which can result in lower fees and expenses. This means that investors can potentially keep more of their returns over the long-term. Diversification: Buffett has also emphasized the importance of diversification in building a successful investment portfolio. By investing in a broad range of stocks or bonds, investors can potentially reduce their risk and avoid the negative impacts of market fluctuations on any single investment. Index funds are designed to provide this diversification, as they typically invest in a wide range of stocks or bonds. Long-term focus: Buffett has long advocated for taking a long-term view when investing in the stock market, and index funds are designed for long-term investing. By tracking a specific market index over a period of years or even decades, index funds can potentially provide investors with significant wealth creation over time. Market returns: Buffett has emphasized the importance of investing in the stock market, rather than trying to pick individual stocks. Since index funds track a specific market index, their returns are generally in line with the overall performance of the market. Over the long-term, the stock market has historically provided strong returns, which can potentially result in significant wealth creation for index fund investors. Consistency: Buffett has also emphasized the importance of consistency in investing. By investing regularly in a low-cost index fund, investors can potentially benefit from the power of compounding and achieve consistent returns over time. This can be particularly valuable for investors who are looking to build wealth over the long-term, as it can help them avoid the pitfalls of short-term market fluctuations. Overall, index funds are a valuable tool for investors looking to build long-term wealth, and Warren Buffett's endorsement of index funds underscores their potential value. By keeping costs low, providing diversification, focusing on the long-term, and investing in the stock market, index funds can potentially help investors achieve their investment goals over time. Index funds can be a valuable tool for building long-term wealth, but they are not a guaranteed path to riches. Like any investment strategy, the potential for wealth creation with index funds depends on a variety of factors, including market conditions, investment goals, and risk tolerance. Here are some of the ways that index funds can potentially help investors build wealth over the long-term: Low costs: One of the primary advantages of index funds is their low expense ratios. Since they are designed to track a specific market index, they require less management and research than actively managed funds. This means that investors pay lower fees, which can potentially result in higher returns over the long-term. Diversification: Index funds typically invest in a broad range of stocks or bonds, which can provide investors with exposure to a diverse array of industries and sectors. By diversifying across multiple stocks or bonds, investors can potentially reduce their risk and avoid the negative impacts of market fluctuations on any single investment. Long-term focus: Index funds are designed for long-term investing and are intended to track a specific market index over a period of years or even decades. By taking a long-term view, investors can potentially benefit from the power of compounding, as their investments grow over time. Market returns: Since index funds track a specific market index, their returns are generally in line with the overall performance of the market. Over the long-term, the stock market has historically provided strong returns, which can potentially result in significant wealth creation for index fund investors. However, it is important to note that index funds are not a guaranteed path to riches. Like any investment strategy, there are risks associated with index fund investing, including market volatility and the potential for losses. Additionally, index funds may not be appropriate for all investors, particularly those with a shorter investment horizon or a higher risk tolerance. While they are designed for long-term investing, they may not be the best choice for investors who need to access their funds in the short-term or who have a low tolerance for risk. Ultimately, the potential for index funds to make investors rich depends on a variety of factors, including market conditions, investment goals, and risk tolerance. While they can be a valuable tool for building long-term wealth, it is important for investors to carefully evaluate their individual circumstances and consult with a financial advisor before making any investment decisions.

Chapter 17
7 Human Relationships

Warren Buffett, one of the most successful investors of all time, is known not only for his financial acumen but also for his wisdom on human relationships. Here are some of his notable quotes on the subject: "It takes 20 years to build a reputation and five minutes to ruin it. If you think about that, you'll do things differently." Buffett emphasizes the importance of building and maintaining a good reputation, both in business and in personal relationships. He emphasizes the need to act with integrity and honesty in all interactions, as trust is a key element in building successful relationships. "In looking for people to hire, look for three qualities: integrity, intelligence, and energy. And if they don't have the first one, the other two will kill you." Buffett emphasizes the importance of hiring people with strong character and values, as these qualities are essential to building a successful team. "It's better to hang out with people better than you. Pick out associates whose behavior is better than yours and you'll drift in that direction." Buffett stresses the importance of surrounding oneself with people who inspire and challenge us to be better, both personally and professionally. "The best thing I did was choose the right heroes." Buffett emphasizes the importance of having positive role models and learning from their successes and failures. "The most important investment you can make is in yourself." Buffett emphasizes the importance of investing in oneself through education, personal development, and building relationships. He encourages individuals to continuously learn and grow, both professionally and personally. "It's better to be trusted than to be liked." Buffett emphasizes the importance of building trust in relationships, both in business and in personal interactions. He believes that trust is essential to building successful and lasting relationships. "You only have to do a very few things right in your life so long as you don't do too many things wrong." Buffett stresses the importance of focusing on what truly matters in life and avoiding distractions that can lead to mistakes or missteps. Overall, Warren Buffett's wisdom on human relationships emphasizes the importance of honesty, integrity, trust, and personal growth in building successful relationships. By focusing on these values and qualities, individuals can potentially build strong and lasting relationships, both in business and in their personal lives. Networking and building relationships are important in any industry, and stock investing is no exception. Here are some ways that networking and building relationships can help investors achieve success in the stock market: Access to information: Networking and building relationships can provide investors with access to information that they may not have otherwise. By connecting with other investors, industry professionals, and analysts, investors can potentially gain insights into market trends, company news, and other factors that may impact stock prices. Collaborative opportunities: Building relationships with other investors can create opportunities for collaboration, such as pooling resources to invest in a particular stock or sharing research and analysis. Collaborating with others can potentially increase the chances of success and reduce the risk of individual mistakes. Diversification: Networking and building relationships can help investors diversify their portfolios by connecting with investors who have expertise in different industries or asset classes. This can help investors gain exposure to a broader range of investments and potentially reduce risk. Mentorship and guidance: Networking and building relationships with experienced investors can provide newer investors with valuable mentorship and guidance. Experienced investors can offer insights and advice on investing strategies, risk management, and other important topics. Access to capital: Building relationships with investors, particularly those with significant financial resources, can provide access to capital that may be needed to make larger investments or take advantage of investment opportunities. Brand building: Networking and building relationships can also help investors build their personal brand and reputation within the industry. By establishing a reputation as a knowledgeable and trustworthy investor, individuals may attract more investment opportunities and potentially increase their returns. Some ways to network and build relationships in the stock investing industry include - Joining investment clubs or groups: Investment clubs and groups provide opportunities to connect with other investors and share research and analysis. Attending conferences and seminars: Industry events such as conferences and seminars provide opportunities to connect with other investors, analysts, and industry professionals. Utilizing social media: Social media platforms such as LinkedIn and Twitter can be used to connect with other investors and industry professionals, share insights and analysis, and build a personal brand. Seeking mentorship and guidance: Experienced investors can provide valuable mentorship and guidance on investing strategies, risk management, and other important topics. Collaborating with others: Collaborating with other investors can provide opportunities to pool resources, share insights, and potentially increase the chances of success. In summary, networking and building relationships are important in stock investing as they can provide access to information, collaborative opportunities, diversification, mentorship and guidance, access to capital, and opportunities to build a personal brand. By actively seeking out opportunities to network and build relationships within the industry, investors can potentially increase their chances of success in the stock market. Investing in a mentor can be a valuable way to gain knowledge and guidance in a particular field or industry. While it may require an initial investment of time and resources, the benefits of working with a mentor can potentially lead to long-term success and growth. Here are some reasons why it may be worth investing in a mentor: Experience and Expertise: A mentor can offer valuable experience and expertise in a particular field or industry that can be difficult to acquire on your own. Mentors can provide insights and knowledge that can help you make better decisions, avoid common pitfalls, and identify new opportunities. Networking: Mentors often have extensive networks of contacts within their industry, which can provide valuable connections and opportunities for professional growth. Working with a mentor can give you access to these networks and help you build your own professional network. Accountability: A mentor can help keep you accountable to your goals and commitments, which can be especially valuable if you are starting a new venture or trying to make significant changes in your career. Mentors can provide guidance, support, and feedback to help you stay on track and make progress towards your goals. Personal Development: Working with a mentor can also contribute to your personal development by helping you identify your strengths and weaknesses and develop strategies for improvement. Mentors can provide feedback and support to help you become a more effective communicator, leader, and problem solver. Faster Learning Curve: By working with a mentor, you can potentially accelerate your learning curve and achieve greater success in a shorter amount of time. Mentors can help you avoid common mistakes and provide guidance on how to achieve your goals more efficiently. While investing in a mentor can have many benefits, it's important to carefully evaluate potential mentors before committing to a mentoring relationship. Some factors to consider include their experience and expertise in your field, their availability and willingness to invest time and resources in your growth, and their communication style and personality. In addition, it's important to have a clear understanding of your own goals and expectations for the mentoring relationship. What specific areas do you want to improve on? How do you want the mentor to help you achieve your goals? What are your expectations in terms of time commitment and communication? Overall, investing in a mentor can be a valuable way to accelerate your growth and achieve greater success in your career or business. By carefully evaluating potential mentors and setting clear goals and expectations, you can maximize the benefits of this investment and achieve your full potential. The 3 As of mentorship are the key qualities that make a great mentor. These qualities are essential for building a strong and effective mentor-mentee relationship that can lead to personal and professional growth. The three As are - Availability: A good mentor is available and willing to invest time and effort into the mentoring relationship. Availability means being responsive to the mentee's needs, providing regular feedback and guidance, and making time for regular meetings or check-ins. Affability: Affability refers to the mentor's ability to build a positive and supportive relationship with the mentee. A good mentor should be approachable, empathetic, and supportive, creating an environment in which the mentee feels comfortable asking questions, seeking advice, and discussing their goals and challenges. Ability: Ability refers to the mentor's expertise and knowledge in the field or industry in which the mentee is seeking guidance. A good mentor should have a deep understanding of the industry, as well as the skills and experience necessary to provide relevant and practical advice to the mentee. These three qualities work together to create a successful mentor-mentee relationship. Without availability, the mentor may not be able to provide the necessary support and guidance to the mentee. Without affability, the mentee may not feel comfortable seeking advice or discussing their challenges. And without ability, the mentor may not have the expertise and knowledge necessary to provide relevant and effective guidance. The 3

As of mentorship are not just important for mentors, but also for mentees. Mentees should seek out mentors who demonstrate these qualities and strive to develop these qualities themselves in order to be effective mentors in their own right. Here are some additional tips for building a successful mentor-mentee relationship: Set clear expectations: Both the mentor and mentee should have a clear understanding of what they hope to achieve through the mentoring relationship. This includes specific goals, expectations for communication and feedback, and the time commitment required. Be open and honest: Both the mentor and mentee should be open and honest about their goals, challenges, and expectations for the mentoring relationship. This includes being willing to give and receive feedback, and being open to constructive criticism. Stay engaged: Both the mentor and mentee should remain engaged and committed to the mentoring relationship over the long term. This includes making time for regular check-ins, following through on commitments, and maintaining a positive and supportive relationship. In summary, the 3 As of mentorship are availability, affability, and ability. These qualities are essential for building a successful mentor-mentee relationship and achieving personal and professional growth. By setting clear expectations, being open and honest, and staying engaged, both mentors and mentees can create a productive and rewarding mentoring relationship that benefits everyone involved.

Chapter 18
Risky Business

Investing in stocks can be a risky venture, and it's not always possible to predict when a stock investment may fail. However, there are certain factors that investors can look for to identify potential risks and make more informed investment decisions. Here are some things to look for in a stock investment before it fails: Financials: One of the most important factors to consider when investing in a stock is the company's financials. Investors should look at the company's revenue growth, profitability, debt levels, and cash flow to ensure that the company is financially stable and has a sustainable business model. Industry trends: It's important to consider broader industry trends and economic conditions that may impact a company's performance. For example, if a company operates in a sector that is facing declining demand or increasing competition, it may be at risk of failing. Management: The quality of a company's management team is another important factor to consider. Investors should look for a management team that has a track record of success, is transparent in its communications, and has a clear strategy for growth. Competitive advantage: A company's competitive advantage, or its ability to differentiate itself from competitors, is another important factor to consider. Investors should look for companies that have a unique value proposition, strong brand recognition, or other factors that make them less susceptible to competition. Valuation: Investors should carefully consider the valuation of a stock before investing. If a stock is trading at a high price relative to its earnings or other metrics, it may be overvalued and at risk of declining in value. Regulatory risks: Certain industries, such as healthcare or financial services, may be subject to increased regulatory scrutiny that can impact a company's performance. Investors should be aware of these risks and consider them when evaluating a potential investment. Company culture: A company's culture and reputation can also impact its long-term success. Investors should look for companies that have a strong ethical culture and are committed to sustainability and social responsibility. In summary, there are several factors that investors should consider when evaluating a potential stock investment. By focusing on factors such as financials, industry trends, management, competitive advantage, valuation, regulatory risks, and company culture, investors can potentially identify stocks that are less likely to fail and make more informed investment decisions. However, it's important to remember that investing always carries some level of risk, and even the most thorough analysis cannot guarantee success. Investing comes with various risks that investors need to be aware of. While there are no guarantees when it comes to investing, understanding the risks can help investors make more informed decisions. Here are the four main risks of investing: Market risk: Market risk, also known as systematic risk, refers to the risk of losses due to changes in the overall market. This can include factors such as changes in interest rates, economic conditions, or geopolitical events that impact the market. Market risk cannot be eliminated through diversification and affects all investments to some degree. Credit risk: Credit risk refers to the risk of a borrower failing to make interest payments or repay the principal amount of a loan. This risk is more relevant for fixed income investments such as bonds but can also affect other investments such as stocks. Companies that are highly leveraged or have poor credit ratings are more susceptible to credit risk. Inflation risk: Inflation risk refers to the risk of losing purchasing power over time due to rising inflation. If the return on an investment does not keep pace with inflation, the investor's purchasing power will be eroded. This risk is particularly relevant for fixed income investments such as bonds or savings accounts that offer low returns. Specific risk: Specific risk, also known as unsystematic risk, refers to the risk of losses due to factors specific to a particular company or investment. This can include factors such as management changes, industry disruptions, or company-specific events such as product recalls or lawsuits. Specific risk can be reduced through diversification, as it affects individual investments rather than the market. To manage these risks, investors should carefully consider their investment objectives, time horizon, and risk tolerance before making any investment decisions. Diversification can also help reduce specific risk by spreading investments across multiple companies and asset classes. Additionally, investors should regularly review their investments and adjust their portfolios as necessary to reflect changing market conditions and their personal financial goals. While investing comes with risks, taking a disciplined and informed approach can help investors achieve their long-term financial objectives. Understanding these risks can help investors make informed decisions and manage their portfolios. Here are ten risks that stocks face: Market Risk: This refers to the risk of losing value due to overall market fluctuations. Stocks are influenced by the broader economy, interest rates, and geopolitical events that can impact the entire market. This risk is unavoidable and affects all investments to some degree. Company-Specific Risk: This refers to the risk of losing value due to factors specific to the company, such as poor management, declining sales, or product recalls. Company-specific risk can be mitigated by diversification but cannot be eliminated entirely. Industry Risk: This refers to the risk of losing value due to factors specific to the industry, such as regulatory changes or increased competition. Investing in a diversified portfolio of stocks across different industries can help mitigate industry-specific risk. Liquidity Risk: This refers to the risk of not being able to sell a stock at a reasonable price due to low trading volume or limited market interest. This risk is more relevant for small-cap stocks or stocks that are less actively traded. Interest Rate Risk: This refers to the risk of losing value due to changes in interest rates. Stocks are particularly sensitive to interest rate changes, as higher interest rates can make stocks less attractive compared to other investments such as bonds. Currency Risk: This refers to the risk of losing value due to changes in currency exchange rates. For example, if an investor holds a foreign stock that is denominated in a different currency, changes in exchange rates can impact the value of the investment. Political Risk: This refers to the risk of losing value due to changes in government policies or instability in a particular country or region. This risk is more relevant for companies that operate in politically sensitive regions or industries. Default Risk: This refers to the risk of losing value due to a company defaulting on its debt or obligations. This risk is more relevant for companies that are heavily indebted or have poor credit ratings. Systemic Risk: This refers to the risk of a major economic or financial crisis that impacts the entire market. For example, the 2008 financial crisis was a systemic risk that impacted stocks across all industries and sectors. Volatility Risk: This refers to the risk of losing value due to fluctuations in the stock price. While volatility is a natural part of investing, investors who are risk-averse may want to avoid stocks with high levels of volatility. In summary, investing in stocks comes with various risks that investors should be aware of. While some risks are unavoidable, diversification and a long-term investment strategy can help mitigate these risks and potentially generate returns over time. It's important for investors to conduct their own research and consult with a financial advisor before making any investment decisions.

Chapter 19
70/30 Rule

The Buffett Rule 70 30 is a popular investment strategy advocated by legendary investor Warren Buffett. This rule suggests that investors allocate 70% of their portfolio to stocks and 30% to bonds. The rationale behind this rule is based on the different risk-return profiles of stocks and bonds. Stocks are generally considered to be riskier investments, but they also offer the potential for higher returns over the long term. On the other hand, bonds are less risky investments, but they typically offer lower returns than stocks. By allocating 70% of a portfolio to stocks and 30% to bonds, investors can potentially benefit from the higher returns of stocks while also minimizing their overall risk through the inclusion of bonds. This strategy is designed to balance the potential for long-term growth with the need for capital preservation and risk management. The 70% allocation to stocks is based on the belief that over the long term, stocks have historically delivered higher returns than other asset classes such as bonds or cash. This is due to the potential for companies to generate profits and grow their earnings over time, which can lead to appreciation in the value of their stocks. However, it's important to note that stocks also come with higher volatility and risk, which can lead to significant fluctuations in the value of a portfolio. The 30% allocation to bonds is designed to provide diversification and stability to a portfolio. Bonds are typically considered to be less risky than stocks, as they offer a fixed income stream and are typically less volatile. By including bonds in a portfolio, investors can potentially reduce the overall risk of their investments and provide a buffer against market downturns. It's important to note that the specific allocation of a portfolio will depend on an investor's individual goals, risk tolerance, and investment time horizon. The 70 30 rule is simply a general guideline that can be used as a starting point for developing an investment strategy. In addition, the 70 30 rule is not a one-size-fits-all strategy, and investors may need to adjust their allocations based on changing market conditions or their individual circumstances. For example, as investors approach retirement, they may want to shift their allocations to a more conservative mix of stocks and bonds in order to minimize the risk of capital loss. Overall, the Buffett Rule 70/30 is a popular investment strategy that is designed to balance the potential for long-term growth with the need for capital preservation and risk management. By allocating 70% of a portfolio to stocks and 30% to bonds, investors can potentially benefit from the higher returns of stocks while also minimizing their overall risk through the inclusion of bonds. However, it's important to note that the specific allocation of a portfolio will depend on an investor's individual goals, risk tolerance, and investment time horizon, and should be carefully considered before making any investment decisions. However, despite his reputation for long-term investing, Buffett has also been known to recommend short-term bonds as a component of a well-diversified investment portfolio. One of the main reasons why Buffett recommends short-term bonds is that they provide a relatively low-risk way to earn a steady stream of income. Short-term bonds typically have maturities of less than five years, which means that they are less exposed to interest rate fluctuations than longer-term bonds. This can make them a good choice for investors who are looking for a relatively stable source of income, without taking on excessive risk. In addition to providing income, short-term bonds can also serve to manage risk in a portfolio. By including short-term bonds in a portfolio, investors can potentially reduce the overall risk of their investments and provide a buffer against market downturns. This is because short-term bonds tend to be less volatile than stocks and longer-term bonds, which can help to stabilize the overall value of a portfolio. Another reason why Buffett recommends short-term bonds is that they can be a useful tool for preserving capital. When interest rates rise, the value of existing bonds typically falls, which can be a concern for investors who are holding longer-term bonds. However, because short-term bonds have relatively short maturities, they are less exposed to interest rate risk than longer-term bonds. This means that investors who hold short-term bonds can potentially avoid some of the capital losses that can occur when interest rates rise.

Finally, Buffett may recommend short-term bonds simply as a matter of personal preference. Buffett is known for his conservative approach to investing, and short-term bonds may align with his overall investment philosophy. By focusing on investments that are relatively low-risk and have a clear path to profitability, Buffett has been able to achieve consistent returns over the long term. Of course, it's important to note that short-term bonds are not without their risks. Like all investments, short-term bonds carry some level of risk, and investors should carefully consider their risk tolerance and investment goals before including short-term bonds in their portfolio. In addition, the specific allocation of a portfolio will depend on an investor's individual circumstances and should be carefully considered before making any investment decision. Warren Buffett recommends short-term bonds to earn a steady stream of income, manage risk, and preserve capital. By including short-term bonds in a well-diversified investment portfolio, investors can potentially achieve consistent returns over the long term, while also minimizing their exposure to market fluctuations and interest rate risk. However, as with all investments, it's important to carefully consider the risks and benefits of short-term bonds before making any investment decisions. Treasury bonds are issued by the U.S. government and are one of the safest investments available, with a low risk of default. Because of this, they are often used as a haven asset during times of economic uncertainty or market volatility. Buffett has stated that he views U.S. Treasuries as a relatively safe investment and has invested in them on occasion. However, he has also noted that the low yields on Treasuries make them less attractive from an investment standpoint, and that he generally prefers to invest in higher-yielding assets such as stocks and corporate bonds. In general, Buffett's investment approach is focused on finding high-quality companies with a strong competitive advantage and a track record of consistent earnings growth. While he may include Treasuries in his portfolio to manage risk or provide a haven during market downturns, they are unlikely to be a significant component of his investment strategy.

Chapter 20
Real Estate Rule

Warren Buffett is one of the most successful investors of all time, and he is known for his contrarian views on many aspects of investing. One area where he has been particularly vocal is real estate, which he has often described as a "lousy investment." While this view may be surprising to many people, there are several reasons why Buffett believes that real estate is not a good investment option. One of the main reasons why Buffett views real estate as a lousy investment is the high transaction costs associated with buying and selling property. These costs include real estate agent commissions, legal fees, inspection costs, and other expenses that can add up quickly. In many cases, these costs can significantly erode any potential profits from a real estate investment. Another problem with real estate as an investment is the lack of liquidity. Unlike stocks or other assets that can be easily bought or sold on an exchange, real estate transactions can take months to complete. This can make it difficult for investors to quickly sell their property if they need to raise cash or adjust their investment portfolio. Real estate investments also tend to be concentrated in a single location or market, which can make it difficult to achieve diversification. Unlike stocks, which can be easily diversified across different sectors and geographic regions, real estate investments are often limited to a single property or location. This can increase the risk of losses if the local real estate market experiences a downturn. Real estate investments also tend to be expensive to maintain, particularly if the property is a rental unit. Landlords must maintain the property, deal with tenants, and cover any expenses that arise, such as repairs or property taxes. These costs can add up quickly, particularly if the property is not generating sufficient rental income. Finally, Buffett has argued that real estate investments may have limited potential for appreciation compared to other assets, such as stocks. While some properties may appreciate over time, this growth is often slow and subject to fluctuations in the local real estate market. In contrast, stocks have historically provided higher rates of return over the long term. While Buffett has been critical of real estate as an investment, it's worth noting that he has made a few successful real estate investments over the years. For example, in the early 2000s, he invested in a group of real estate companies that focused on commercial properties. This investment proved to be very profitable, earning Buffett and his company, Berkshire Hathaway, a significant return. Warren Buffett's view on real estate as a lousy investment is based on several factors, including high transaction costs, lack of liquidity, difficulty in diversification, high maintenance costs, and limited potential for appreciation. While some investors may find success in real estate, it's important to carefully consider the risks and challenges associated with this type of investment. As with all investments, it's important to do your research, carefully evaluate your options, and make informed decisions based on your individual circumstances and investment goals. While he has been critical of real estate as an investment, he has made a few successful real estate investments over the years, including using Real Estate Investment Trusts (REITs). REITs are a type of investment vehicle that allows investors to invest in real estate properties without owning them outright. Instead, REITs pool together funds from multiple investors to purchase and manage real estate properties, such as apartment buildings, office buildings, and shopping centers. REITs are required to distribute at least 90% of their taxable income to investors in the form of dividends, making them a popular choice for income-seeking investors. While Buffett has been critical of real estate as an investment in general, he has not been opposed to investing in REITs. In fact, Berkshire Hathaway has held positions in several REITs over the years, including - STORE Capital Corporation (STOR) In 2017, Berkshire Hathaway made a significant investment in STORE Capital Corporation, a publicly traded REIT that focuses on single-tenant operational real estate. As of 2021, Berkshire Hathaway holds a 17% stake in the company, making it one of the largest shareholders. Seritage Growth Properties (SRG) Seritage Growth Properties is a REIT that owns and manages a portfolio of retail properties, including those formerly owned by Sears Holdings Corporation. Berkshire Hathaway has been a significant shareholder in Seritage since 2015, and as of 2021, holds a 5.8% stake in the company. Equity Residential (EQR) Equity Residential is a REIT that specializes in the ownership and management of apartment buildings. Berkshire Hathaway has held a position in the company since 2006, and as of 2021, holds a 3.7% stake in the company. It's worth noting that while Berkshire Hathaway has held positions in these and other REITs, these investments represent only a small portion of the company's overall portfolio. Berkshire Hathaway's investment strategy is focused primarily on high-quality companies with strong competitive advantages, and while REITs may be a part of that strategy, they are not a major focus. While Warren Buffett has been critical of real estate as an investment in general, he has not been opposed to investing in REITs. Berkshire Hathaway has held positions in several REITs over the years, including STORE Capital Corporation, Seritage Growth Properties, and Equity Residential. However, these investments represent only a small portion of Berkshire Hathaway's overall portfolio, and the company's investment strategy is primarily focused on high-quality companies with strong competitive advantages. Real Estate Investment Trusts (REITs) are a popular investment vehicle for investors looking to gain exposure to the real estate market without the hassle of owning and managing physical properties. While it's difficult to generalize the investment strategies of billionaires, some do invest in REITs as part of their investment portfolio. One notable example is Sam Zell, the founder and chairman of Equity Group Investments. Zell is a billionaire real estate investor and has been a longtime proponent of REITs. He was one of the pioneers of the modern REIT industry and has made significant investments in the space over the years. In fact, he is often referred to as the "father of the modern REIT." Another example is billionaire investor Ken Griffin, the founder, and CEO of Citadel LLC. Griffin has been an active investor in the real estate market for years and has used REITs to gain exposure to the sector. In 2017, Citadel purchased a 5% stake in Invitation Homes, one of the largest single-family home rental companies in the United States. Warren Buffett, one of the most successful investors of all time, has also made investments in REITs over the years. While he has been critical of real estate as an investment in general, he has made significant investments in several REITs, including STORE Capital Corporation, Seritage Growth Properties, and Equity Residential, through his company, Berkshire Hathaway. Other billionaire investors who have invested in REITs include Barry Sternlicht, the founder and CEO of Starwood Capital Group, and Bill Ackman, the founder and CEO of Pershing Square Capital Management. REITs can offer several benefits for investors, including diversification, liquidity, and the potential for stable income. For billionaires and other investors with significant wealth, REITs can be a valuable component of a well-diversified investment portfolio. While it's difficult to generalize the investment strategies of billionaires, some do invest in REITs as part of their investment portfolio. Notable examples include Sam Zell, Ken Griffin, and Warren Buffett. REITs can offer several benefits for investors, including diversification, liquidity, and the potential for stable income. Real Estate Investment Trusts (REITs) are investment vehicles that allow individuals to invest in real estate without owning physical properties. REITs own and operate income-generating properties such as shopping centers, office buildings, and apartment complexes. Here are the top five largest REITs by market capitalization as of 2022: With a market capitalization of over $128 billion, American Tower (AMT) is the largest REIT in the world. It owns and operates wireless communication towers and other infrastructure primarily in the United States, but also in international markets such as India and Brazil. Prologis Inc. (PLD) is the largest industrial REIT in the world, with a market capitalization of over $109 billion. It owns and operates logistics and distribution facilities primarily in the United States, Europe, and Asia. Prologis serves a diverse customer base, including e-commerce retailers, manufacturers, and transportation companies. Crown Castle International Corp. (CCI) is a REIT that owns and operates wireless communication infrastructure primarily in the United States. It has a market capitalization of over $86 billion and owns approximately 40,000 cell towers and 80,000 small cell nodes. Crown Castle's infrastructure supports wireless carriers and other tenants in the telecommunications industry. Equinix Inc. (EQIX) is a REIT that owns and operates data centers around the world. With a market capitalization of over $84 billion, it is the largest data center REIT in the world. Equinix's data centers provide space, power, and connectivity for a variety of customers, including cloud providers, network service providers, and financial services firms. Simon Property Group Inc. (SPG) is the largest retail REIT in the world, with a market capitalization of over $56 billion. It owns and operates shopping malls, premium outlets, and other retail properties primarily in the United States, but also in Europe and Asia. Simon Property Group's properties are leased to a diverse group of retailers and other tenants. These five REITs represent a variety of real estate sectors, including telecommunications infrastructure, industrial properties, data centers, and retail properties. They offer investors exposure to diverse real estate assets and the potential for stable income through dividends. It's worth noting that market capitalization can fluctuate over time, and the top five largest REITs may change over time. Real Estate Investment Trusts (REITs) can be a viable option for building wealth, as they offer investors exposure to income-generating real estate assets without requiring them to purchase and manage properties themselves. Here are some ways REITs can help build wealth: Diversification: REITs offer diversification by investing in a variety of real estate assets, such as shopping centers, office buildings, apartment complexes, and warehouses. This diversification can help reduce overall investment risk and increase the potential for stable income and long-term capital appreciation. Passive Income: REITs generate income through the rental income from their properties, which is then distributed to shareholders in the form of dividends. This passive income can provide a steady stream of cash flow and help build wealth over time. Liquidity: REITs trade on stock exchanges, making them more liquid than physical real estate investments. This means that investors can easily buy and sell shares of REITs as needed, allowing them to adjust their portfolio holdings to meet their financial goals. Professional Management: REITs are managed by experienced real estate professionals, who oversee the day-to-day operations of the properties and work to maximize their value. This allows investors to benefit from the expertise of professionals without having to manage properties themselves. Tax Advantages: REITs are required by law to distribute at least 90% of their taxable income to shareholders in the form of dividends, which are taxed at the shareholder's individual tax rate. This can result in tax advantages for investors, as the dividends are typically taxed at a lower rate than ordinary income. It's important to note that like any investment, REITs do carry risks, such as fluctuations in interest rates, changes in economic conditions, and shifts in real estate markets. It's important to do your research and assess your own risk tolerance before investing in REITs or any other investment vehicle. In addition, it's important to consider the fees associated with investing in REITs, such as management fees and transaction costs. These fees can eat into your returns and should be carefully evaluated before making an investment. Overall, REITs can be a valuable addition to a well-diversified investment portfolio and can help build wealth over the long term. As with any investment, it's important to do your due diligence and assess your own financial situation and goals before investing. Real Estate Investment Trusts (REITs) are a type of investment vehicle that owns and operates income-generating real estate properties. While REITs can offer attractive investment opportunities, they also have some downsides that investors should be aware of before investing. Here are some of the main disadvantages of investing in REITs: Interest Rates: REITs are sensitive to changes in interest rates. When interest rates rise, the cost of borrowing money to acquire or develop real estate increases, which can reduce profitability for REITs. Additionally, rising interest rates can make other investments, such as bonds, more attractive to investors, which can decrease demand for REITs and lower their market value. Market Fluctuations: Like other investments, REITs are subject to market fluctuations and may experience volatility in response to changes in economic conditions or other external factors. This volatility can be particularly pronounced during times of economic uncertainty or instability. Property Values: The value of a REIT's real estate holdings can fluctuate based on changes in market conditions, such as changes in supply and demand or shifts in local real estate markets. Additionally, some types of real estate, such as retail or office space, may be more susceptible to market fluctuations than others, such as healthcare or industrial properties. Tenant Risk: REITs are dependent on tenants to generate rental income, and tenant defaults or vacancies can have a significant impact on a REIT's profitability. Additionally, tenant risk can vary based on the type of property and the tenant's creditworthiness, among other factors. Regulatory Risk: REITs are subject to a variety of regulations, including tax and securities laws. Changes in regulations or tax laws can have a significant impact on the profitability of REITs, and regulatory violations can result in fines or other penalties. Management Risk: REITs are managed by teams of professionals who make decisions about acquiring and developing properties, setting rental rates, and other strategic decisions. Poor management decisions can have a significant impact on the performance of a REIT, and investors should carefully evaluate the experience and track record of a REIT's management team before investing. Fees: Like other investment vehicles, REITs may charge fees to cover management and other expenses. These fees can reduce the overall return on investment and may vary depending on the specific REIT and its management structure. In summary, while REITs can offer attractive investment opportunities, they also have some disadvantages that investors should be aware of. Before investing in REITs, investors should carefully evaluate the risks and potential rewards of these investments and consult with financial professionals to determine whether REITs are an appropriate addition to their investment portfolio.

Conclusion

Warren Buffett is widely considered one of the most successful investors of all time, and his annual letter to shareholders of Berkshire Hathaway is eagerly anticipated by investors and analysts alike. The letter provides valuable insights into Buffett's investment philosophy, as well as his thoughts on the current state of the market and the economy. Here are some key takeaways from Warren Buffett's annual letter: The importance of long-term thinking: Warren Buffett is known for his patient and disciplined approach to investing, and this year's letter underscores the importance of taking a long-term view. Buffett emphasizes that short-term market fluctuations should not distract investors from the long-term potential of their investments. The benefits of a concentrated portfolio: While many investors advocate for diversification, Buffett takes a different approach. He argues that a concentrated portfolio of high-quality stocks can deliver better returns over the long term. However, he emphasizes that this strategy is only appropriate for investors who have a deep understanding of the companies in their portfolio. The value of retained earnings: Buffett has long emphasized the importance of companies reinvesting their earnings to generate long-term growth. In this year's letter, he notes that Berkshire Hathaway has benefitted from the retained earnings of the companies it owns, which have allowed them to reinvest in their businesses and generate strong returns. The risks of overpaying for acquisitions: Buffett notes that Berkshire Hathaway's recent acquisition of Precision Castparts was one of its largest ever, but also one of its riskiest. He emphasizes the importance of being disciplined when it comes to acquisitions and avoiding overpaying for companies, which can lead to poor returns. The challenges of finding attractive investments: With interest rates at historic lows, Buffett notes that it has become increasingly difficult to find attractive investments. He highlights the importance of patience and discipline in waiting for the right opportunities, rather than chasing after high-risk investments. The importance of corporate culture: Buffett emphasizes the importance of corporate culture in driving long-term success. He notes that Berkshire Hathaway looks for companies with strong cultures that align with its values, and that the company's decentralized structure allows for autonomy and innovation. The risks of speculation: Buffett cautions against the dangers of speculation and notes that many investors are drawn to risky investments such as cryptocurrencies and SPACs. He warns that these types of investments are often driven by speculation rather than underlying fundamentals and can lead to significant losses. Overall, Warren Buffett's annual letter provides valuable insights into his investment philosophy and approach to managing Berkshire Hathaway's portfolio. While some of the themes may be familiar to longtime Buffett followers, his observations on the current state of the market and the economy provide important context for investors seeking to navigate an increasingly complex investment landscape. Warren Buffett is one of the most successful investors of all time, with a net worth of over $100 billion. His investing strategy, which he has developed over decades of experience, is centered around the concept of value investing. Here are some key principles of Warren Buffett's investing strategy: Focus on long-term value: Warren Buffett is known for his patient and disciplined approach to investing. He looks for companies that have a strong competitive advantage and can generate sustainable earnings growth over the long term. Rather than trying to time the market or make quick trades, he focuses on the long-term value of his investments. Invest in businesses, not stocks: Buffett sees himself as a business owner, rather than a stock trader. He looks for companies with strong management teams, a clear competitive advantage, and a sustainable business model. He prefers companies that generate high returns on equity and have a strong track record of profitability. Buy stocks at a discount: Buffett's value investing strategy focuses on buying stocks at a discount to their intrinsic value. He looks for companies that are undervalued by the market, either because they are misunderstood or because they are going through a temporary setback. By buying stocks at a discount, he can generate higher returns over the long term.

Diversify intelligently: While some investors advocate for diversification, Buffett takes a different approach. He focuses on investing in a few high-quality companies that he understands well, rather than spreading his investments across many stocks. However, he emphasizes the importance of diversifying intelligently, by investing in companies across different industries and sectors.

Keep costs low: Warren Buffett is known for his frugal lifestyle, and he applies this same principle to his investing strategy. He looks for low-cost investments, such as index funds, and avoids high-fee investments that can eat into returns over the long term. Have a margin of safety: Buffett emphasizes the importance of having a margin of safety when investing. This means buying stocks at a significant discount to their intrinsic value, to protect against potential downside risks. By having a margin of safety, investors can potentially generate higher returns with less risk. Be patient and disciplined: Warren Buffett is a patient investor, and he emphasizes the importance of staying disciplined and sticking to his investment strategy. He is not swayed by short-term market fluctuations or the latest investment fads, and instead focuses on the long-term potential of his investments. Overall, Warren Buffett's investing strategy is focused on buying high-quality businesses at a discount to their intrinsic value and holding them for the long term. By focusing on value, keeping costs low, and staying disciplined, he has been able to generate consistently high returns over the course of his career. While he has made investments in a wide range of asset classes over the years, such as stocks, bonds, and real estate, he has consistently emphasized the importance of investing in equities. Warren Buffett has long been an advocate of investing in low-cost index funds, which are designed to track the performance of a specific market index, such as the S&P 500. In his annual letter to shareholders in 2013, he stated, "My advice to the trustee couldn't be simpler: Put 10% of the cash in short-term government bonds and 90% in a very low-cost S&P 500 index fund." Buffett's rationale for investing in index funds is based on the concept of passive investing, which involves holding a diversified portfolio of stocks and avoiding frequent trading. He believes that passive investing is a simple and effective way to generate consistent returns over the long term, while minimizing risk and keeping costs low. Buffett has also emphasized the importance of investing in companies with a strong competitive advantage, or "economic moat," which can help protect against potential downside risks and generate sustainable earnings growth over the long term. He has highlighted companies such as Coca-Cola, American Express, and Apple as examples of companies with strong competitive advantages. Overall, Warren Buffett's investment philosophy emphasizes the importance of investing in high-quality companies at a reasonable price and holding them for the long term. While he has made a wide range of investments over the years, he has consistently emphasized the value of passive investing in low-cost index funds, as well as investing in companies with strong competitive advantages and sustainable earnings growth. Warren Buffett's famous investment philosophy is summed up in his two rules of investing: Rule No. 1: Never Lose Money, and Rule No. 2: Never Forget Rule No. 1. These rules highlight the importance of minimizing risk in investing and protecting your capital, which are critical to achieving long-term investment success. Here are some key takeaways from these rules: Focus on capital preservation: The first rule of investing is to never lose money. This means that you should prioritize protecting your capital above all else, even if it means sacrificing potential gains. By minimizing your losses, you can help ensure that you have the capital needed to take advantage of new opportunities in the future. Avoid chasing short-term gains: Warren Buffett's investment philosophy is focused on long-term value creation, rather than chasing short-term gains. This means investing in high-quality companies with sustainable earnings growth, rather than trying to make a quick profit on the latest market trend. Be patient and disciplined: To avoid losing money, it's important to be patient and disciplined in your investing. This means avoiding impulsive decisions and sticking to your investment plan, even during periods of market volatility. Diversify your portfolio: One way to minimize the risk of losing money is to diversify your portfolio across a range of asset classes and industries. This can help mitigate the impact of market fluctuations and protect your capital over the long term.

Conduct thorough research: To avoid losing money, it's important to conduct thorough research on any investment opportunity. This means analyzing a company's financial statements, assessing its competitive position, and evaluating its growth potential. Manage risk effectively: While it's impossible to eliminate risk from investing, it's important to manage risk effectively to avoid losing money. This means setting appropriate stop-loss limits, using position-sizing strategies, and avoiding investments that are too risky for your portfolio. Stay disciplined during market downturns: During market downturns, it can be tempting to panic and sell off your investments to avoid further losses. However, Warren Buffett advises against this approach, arguing that it's important to stay disciplined and maintain a long-term focus, even during challenging times. In summary, Warren Buffett's two rules of investing highlight the importance of minimizing risk and protecting your capital to achieve long-term investment success. By focusing on capital preservation, avoiding short-term gains, being patient and disciplined, diversifying your portfolio, conducting thorough research, managing risk effectively, and staying disciplined during market downturns, you can help ensure that you never lose money in your investments. Investing in stocks can be a powerful way to build long-term wealth and achieve financial goals. Stocks represent ownership in publicly traded companies, and their value can fluctuate based on a variety of factors, including company performance, economic trends, and market conditions. Here are some of the key benefits of investing in stocks: Potential for long-term growth: Historically, stocks have provided higher long-term returns than other types of investments, such as bonds or cash. While there is no guarantee of future returns, investing in a diversified portfolio of stocks can help to provide potential for long-term growth and wealth accumulation. Diversification: Investing in stocks can help to diversify your portfolio and spread your risk across a range of companies and industries. This can help to reduce the impact of individual company performance or market fluctuations on your overall portfolio. Liquidity: Stocks are generally more liquid than other types of investments, such as real estate or private equity. This means that you can buy and sell shares of stocks relatively easily, allowing you to quickly adjust your portfolio as market conditions change. Income potential: Many stocks pay dividends, which can provide a source of regular income for investors. This can be particularly attractive for retirees or those seeking to generate passive income. Control: Unlike other types of investments, such as mutual funds or exchange-traded funds (ETFs), investing in individual stocks allows you to have more control over your portfolio. You can choose which stocks to buy and sell, and adjust your portfolio based on your own investment goals and risk tolerance. While there are many benefits to investing in stocks, there are also risks considering. The value of stocks can be volatile and can fluctuate based on a variety of factors, including company performance, economic trends, and market conditions. Additionally, investing in individual stocks requires a significant amount of research and analysis to make informed decisions, which may not be suitable for all investors. Here are some key tips for investing in stocks: Diversify your portfolio: Investing in a range of stocks across different companies and industries can help to spread your risk and reduce the impact of individual company performance or market fluctuations on your overall portfolio. Do your research: Before investing in any stock, it's important to conduct thorough research and analysis to understand the company's financial performance, management team, competitive landscape, and growth prospects. Have a long-term perspective: Investing in stocks is generally a long-term strategy, and it's important to have a patient and disciplined approach. Short-term fluctuations in stock prices should not drive your investment decisions. Consider your risk tolerance: Investing in stocks involves risk, and it's important to understand your own risk tolerance and invest accordingly. Consider factors such as your age, investment goals, and financial situation when determining your portfolio allocation. In summary, investing in stocks can provide potential for long-term growth, diversification, liquidity, income, and control over your portfolio. While there are risks considering, a disciplined and informed approach to investing in stocks can help to build long-term wealth and achieve financial goals.